To Janice
May you find this book a source of inspiration in the many journeys of life
Adera Emmanuel "Gorda"

FRAGMENTS OF A FRACTURED LIFE

OVERCOMING PERSONAL TRAUMA, PRIVATE PAIN AND HEALING FORWARD

ADERA GORDON

authorHOUSE®

AuthorHouse™
1663 Liberty Drive, Suite 200
Bloomington, IN 47403
www.authorhouse.com
Phone: 1-800-839-8640

© *2008 Adera Gordon. All rights reserved.*

No part of this book may be reproduced, stored in a retrieval system, or transmitted by any means without the written permission of the author.

First published by AuthorHouse 9/25/2008

ISBN: 978-1-4343-5177-7 (sc)
ISBN: 978-1-4389-0650-8 (hc)

Library of Congress Control Number: 2008906513

Printed in the United States of America
Bloomington, Indiana

This book is printed on acid-free paper.

Note to Readers

We live in a world of many human differences that will forever shape and transform our lives. As you read this story, please keep in mind that this story is not about any one culture, as it is more to do with human circumstances, the challenges we face and the difficult decisions we sometimes have to make. This story is not a depiction of any one culture or people of a certain group. This is a relatable event that can be applied to most families. Perhaps, if not you personally, this story may be relevant to someone in your family or circle of friends. This seems representative of the societies in which we find ourselves; it is about daily struggles and overcoming some of life's challenges.

This work is a memoir reflecting the author's recollection of events and experiences over a period of years. Names, locations, and certain characteristics in this story have been changed to protect the identities of those involved. Some conversations and events have been recreated from memory and translated into English; they are not intended to be an exact representation of past dialogues. In some cases, dialogues have been compressed to convey the substance of the events as they occurred.

Dedication

To my two lovely daughter's and my husband for giving me the strength and courage to tell my story—one that many girls and women like me face daily as we look beyond the shadows of the past in an attempt to live a normal life. I am thankful to have this opportunity to tell about an all-too-familiar experience—a shameful epidemic of sexual abuse that has plagued many communities, yet so few persons are encouraged to tell their stories. I am grateful for the support of my family and their ever-so-delicate nudging me toward the light so that I could see the brightness of the future.

To all survivors of sexual and physical traumas, my wish is that you find peace, beauty, and strength to live another day.

To the fallen angels of this tragic epidemic—those who have succumbed to shame; guilt and have been swallowed by the nightmares. I hope you have found your peace in heaven.

Preface

I wrote this book with several thoughts in mind—to give a voice to my readers, survivors of sexual trauma and domestic violence, so they might feel encouraged to tell their own stories. In sharing my story, I hope to unify our cry, to help put an end to our suffering; and by casting a small stone into the ocean, hopefully a mighty ripple might emerge for the necessary changes in our community; especially when it comes to dealing with and handling sexual crimes, particularly against children. In creating a wave-and-ripple effect, only then will our society realize the grave epidemic of violence against women and children.

As a survivor, I understand the shackles that once held me prisoner and trapped my voice so that I would not speak my truth. We are all responsible for helping to chip away the shackles, until the chains are completely broken. Today, as I look beyond my experiences, I am reflective of the shame and guilt, which have taught me, although, it is not always easy to reveal the details or figure out what would come next after facing such a traumatic existence; what is important, it that we are here!

To all the women and girls who have not had the courage to face their nightmares of sexual abuse and physical violence in a relationship, I embrace you, because for more than thirty years, I kept silent due to fears and the shame of what had been done to me.

Today, still there are those who are trying to suppress my voice for fear that I might offend those who caused me great harm, and the more I feel forced to silence my voice, to change and redirect my experiences so that I may continue to protect the identity of the criminals, the more incensed I feel. I am angry for being made to feel as though I had committed the crimes, for wanting to speak my truth—tell others how I was violently raped and sexually molested as a child. I am incensed for being made to feel as though I were the criminals, when I was only an innocent child who had fallen prey to a violent epidemic.

There are those who have asked me to produce documentations to validate my claim. They've insisted that they have the right to choose how my story, as they attempt to protect the identities of those men who so violently wounded me, who, out of fear, may want to challenge my truth, demanding the right to protect their good names. To them I say, I too, would have liked to have protected my innocence. Now I'm trying to regain what is left of my dignity, self-esteem, self-respect, and—most of all—what is left of my voice.

My objective in speaking out is not in ruining anyone else's life; because you see; I am already a victim of a ruined existence! When I look around and hear the voices of my spiritual sisters—those women and young girls, young boys and children who have shared their encounters of molestation and sexual abuse, whose experiences are uniquely familiar—their voices have continued to be suppressed. I am reclaiming the right to speak out about this violent epidemic in hope of liberating someone else to speak out.

For those who continue to look for documentations, look around and notice the many emotionally broken and devastated spirits. Unfortunately, I don't have any tangible documentation as evidence of my pain, or my injuries. My only documentation is that of a dark past, my internal pain, emotional scars, and the memories that are evident to me and to those who have shared my journey. My documentations are my shame, guilt, fears, and nightmares I have carried for more than thirty years, and the invisible scars that others cannot see. The documentations that are being sought are my lingering sufferings, my efforts to shield the hurt, and the constant feelings of inadequacy.

Today, I stand as a survivor of childhood sexual trauma and of cruel conducts against my innocence. If my emotional scars are insufficient to grant me the right to speak my truth, when will I earn the right to be free of my burdens? If I live in fear of speaking out, how might I give a voice or strength to my children to take a stand, to speak out against what they may know to be wrong? I no longer live in the shadows of the past, and no longer afraid of calling out my molesters, sexual abusers, and kidnappers. I'm not afraid of offending them, if my speaking out saves one innocent child, one young girl, one young boy or a woman from falling victim to abuse; should I offend them—the rapists, the batterers, and the molesters! So be it.

Those who have violated me no longer own the right to continue to silence my voice. I am reminded everyday of the work yet to be accomplished, and the forum yet to be established to give survivors a foundation from which they may speak their truths. I stand in the light signifying that, one day, our voices will be heard much louder across the nation in order to put a stop to these crimes.

Acknowledgements

I am grateful to my mother for instilling in me a great desire and determination to be more than myself, and for never allowing me to see myself as poor, even when the visuals were visibly undesirable. Thank you for your courage in creating resources where there weren't any, and for teaching me the importance of hard work, strength, resilience and independence no matter the circumstance. I am grateful to my father for giving hope and courage.

To my brothers and sisters, far too many to name each and every one of you, thank you for being in my life, and for being the people you were raised to be; for embracing one another, and for treating one another with kindness, love, and respect.

To my dearest friend of twenty-five years, thank you for being a phenomenal sister-friend and for always providing me with a shoulder to lean on.

To my in-laws who have graciously embraced my children and me and have been a tremendous and positive influence in our lives.

In loving memory of Uncle Herman, who provided me with guidance and protection while living in this scary world, and for seeing the need and responding to be that father figure I needed in my life.

In loving memory of my *Grandmère* Carol, whose life ended so suddenly, and from whom I learned humility and compassion.

Forward

My voice was something that I always hoped to find, but as a child, that voice was taken from me. I have lived in the shadows of a timid and bashful girl with a horrible, shameful secret. Now, I find myself with the burning desire to chase away the darkness. I have spent most of my adult life feeling lost—unable to understand the world around me, and unable to comprehend why the wounds that were cut so deeply still hadn't healed. No matter how many ways I tried patching them up, and regardless of how many Band-Aids I applied to cover the gaping holes, they only seem to have gotten wider.

From the outside looking in, very few people would classify me as a victim of any kind, but the confidence I have displayed over the years were simply that of a veil concealing the dark hole that took hold of me. Beneath my mask laid another side that very few people knew about; the other side that was rarely revealed, and reserved only for a privileged few. My calm, easygoing demeanor was fraught with secrets—secrets that threatened the very life I had fought so hard to create for my family.

The angers that were bottled up for so many years and tucked away--the secrets I had hoped would never see the light of day, were eventually spilling over ever so slowly. They were so gradual, that sometimes I forgot they existed. It was only after my babies came— when they started asking questions about my past, my childhood, and about my life— that the suppressed angers again surfaced. Before, I dared not speak of the experiences with anyone—not even them. I was cautious to avoid anything that might have triggered the pain. I went on with life as though nothing had ever happened; living in a complete state of denial, in a state of pretense about how wonderful life was. The truth of the matter was that the memories weren't so wonderful. The secrets of those horrible things, which in all certainty were my reality; I never allowed them to become part of my seemingly ideal world.

Many years after, the angers I felt remained dormant, hibernating, waiting for the opportunity to appear and remind me every so often that they were in control. The shameful reality I had been hiding was still controlling me. It was not until after the birth of my first child, that I realized how damaged I had been inside; how much my heart and mind had been derailed, dying from a lack of oxygen, and my inability to speak of the past.

Over time, the damages became more apparent—my violent rage, the constant screaming, loss of temper, feeling out of control, and lashing out at innocent precious children. The many years of unspoken words and violent images were slowly festering from small droplets to mighty rivers. The bottled-up angers had begun emerging in ways that threatened the relationships I wanted to have with my children now and in the future. I was witnessing and slowly reliving a suffocating history.

I couldn't understand why I would become so enraged with my daughters—my sweet angels; the people I loved most, and the precious gifts who had given my life so much meaning. Most of my anger seemed directed at my oldest child. It was baffling that simple words from her lips would send me into a tangent. I couldn't see that the problem resided within me, my destructive past. It was easier to play the blaming game, accusing my daughter of requiring too much of my attention, and of being too high maintenance. I couldn't understand why I was resentful and envious of my own daughter, who was too young to understand my adverse actions. I couldn't understand why I often felt drained of emotion when I had to give her of myself and of my time. I felt I had very little love and patience left to give. It was far beyond my comprehension that the rages I had displayed toward her were the direct result of my past. Unresolved issues manifesting in destructive actions directed toward my family.

Over the years and after having my second child, I thought my children would be safe from harm, particularly because I had moved far away across state, from those who had caused me so much pain, and although my abusers no longer posed direct physical threats to my life or my children, their imprints continues to impact everyone around me and are forever etched in my core. I have lived with the shame and guilt of what they had done. Unable to speak of their deeds for fear of retaliation, fear of reliving the painful memories and fear of what people would say—that it was my fault, and that I was to blame.

I didn't know how to speak of their deeds, because no one in my family had ever spoken of such deeds. Talks of abuse were never part of our discussions at home, especially the sexual deeds. Yes, there were the occasional talks of the beatings they had received as children—the same beatings I had received and had accepted that such beatings were customarily the way people in my culture disciplined their children. The beatings were something that was as much a part of my culture as a stamp to a letter. The beatings were something that I was accustomed to getting, day after day. If a week went by without getting a one, I would wonder if something was wrong; but the other kinds of abuse--sexual abuse were unspoken taboos.

Most of my adult life, I never knew the correct names to call their crimes, I figured that since I had no names for them, they didn't matter. I believed and rationalized that what was unspoken was easily forgotten, but I couldn't have been more wrong. What I learned over the years was that those unspoken taboos manifest themselves in other ways. It was not until more than twenty years later that I realized the impact of the grave injustice against me.

It has been nearly ten years since my mysterious past was revealed to me in its truest form, until then, I had been in the dark about the extent of the crimes and the severity of the damage. The light was switched on for me when one of the most respected figure in my life, the most famous face on television, told the world of her own experience with sexual abuse. It was at that moment I realized that what had happened to me decades ago was no small matter. Now, I had a name for the crimes they had committed. Suddenly I had a descriptions for what they had done to me. Finally, I realized I was no longer alone.

It was the way she described the acts, peeling away the layers as if peeling an onion. It was the way she broke it down to an elementary level that even a four-year-old would understand the distinctions. It was the way she put the differences into context for me; the way she explained the acts. It was the way she dissected the very differences between molestation and rape. Before I came to understand the true distinction and meaning of what happened, I thought the words were used interchangeably. It was then that I decided to embark on my own journey of healing and forgiveness, so that I would live a freer life—what was left of it—for me and for the people I love and come to terms with speaking my truth.

All the years of rejecting the truth, my reality had become a thing of the past. Today, I am fighting to reclaim the life that was meant for me—the life that was mine to live. Although I understand that my healing wouldn't come without reliving the past, I needed to uncap the bottle and allow the liquids of my memories to flow freely. I believe that in sharing my story; I can heal my own wounds and help others to heal as well. I can help my daughters understand the demons that once lurked behind my composed smile, and the nightmares that had been part of all our lives.

It has become my hope that my daughters and other young women will grow and evolve from my experiences without repeating the pain, suffering, hurt, and history.

Today, I am working toward healing, I am slowly moving away from the guilt and shame; and slowly unloading the heavy burden that once weighed down my heart; I'm slowly releasing the rage toward my abusers. Although I'm still filled with sadness, I'm no longer bitter. I'm hopeful and slowly working towards forgiveness, and I'm slowly learning to accept the past, but without ever forgetting the journey.

In sharing my journey and triumphs, it is my hope to give strength, a voice, and courage to others. It's my way of telling the abusers that I get to have the last word—to show them that my destiny is not what they attempted to make of me, but what I chose to make of myself, regardless of what they had done. I'm reclaiming the life that was once stolen from me, and standing victorious to the end.

The future cannot be accomplished without first understanding the past. I must make that journey one final time.

Journey

We have all taken unforgettable journeys.
Each will forever shape our lives.
Each experience will be different from one to the next.
The question is not always to understand why we take these journeys,
but what lessons we have learned in the passing.
Our journeys, voluntary or involuntary, are our teachers.
Positive or negative, there is something to be gained by all.
The outcome most often depends on our ability to navigate our compass, and our minds.
Dare I ask your direction?
What path will you follow? Where will your compass lead you?
Will you be the sinking ship or the thriving vessel?
Will you succumb to or survive the storms?

Love and peace,
Adera

I

IMPRINTS

He was a young, vibrant, twenty-three-year-old. He had a way with words and persuasion that would convince a corpse it was still alive. He charmed everyone who crossed his path, including me.

Fortunately, for him, when we met, my life felt like that of a corpse—cold, miserable, and dark. For much of my young life, I lived emotionally and physically numb, craving attention from almost anyone who was willing to offer it. Yet, although I hungered for it, my experiences taught me to be very selective of the person I gave my time. In my mind, the lucky guy had to meet certain conditions, and boy, did he meet them all. He was good-looking, charming, funny, and charismatic, to say the least.

My life was like that of a walking dead, and it was not until that midsummer evening, when I looked into his brown, captivating eyes, that I realized I had not lived. He was a smooth talker, he said all the right things—all the things that a broken girl like me would want to hear. He said all the right words that made my heart jump unnaturally, and all the things that seemed possible. In him, I saw a happier life and a happier future.

I was instantly hypnotized by his charms and wanted to be possessed by him, and he didn't disappoint. I wanted to be all that he wanted me to be; I wanted to matter to him, to be a part of something good—be a part of the love and excitement shared by two people. The kind of love I often saw dramatized on television. I wanted to experience the passion I often read about in the Harlequin romance novels; to give him my heart and feel the earth shatter beneath my feet. Naively, I wanted to be part of his world.

We had an instant connection that felt natural and exciting. He had won my heart. I thought it would be enough to give of myself, and in return, he would fill me with the substance I craved most—his love. I believed that he would rid me of the hungers of years past. He offered all that I wanted and more, including an occasional love tap, which he would justify to be loves play.

He was like no other young man I had ever met--not that I met many. He was like the ones I dreamed and fantasized about, the ones who never gave me the time of day, and although he was not the first handsome young man to have captured my heart, he was certainly the first to capture my soul. He made me believe that there was no other girl as special as me. He was not fazed by my dark complexion, as so many others had been.

To him, my darkness wasn't an issue. In fact, he would always tell me how beautiful I was—the darker, the better, he would say. He told me that he was attracted to my inner beauty, not just my exterior, by which so many before him judged my worth. He made me believe that my beauty was skin deep.

Until we met, I had not lived. I had never felt that way about anyone, no one had ever made me feel more beautiful, and no one had ever made me feel more alive or as special as he did. To an already broken lantern looking to be fixed, he seemed to be the person to mend the wounds of my broken heart. He knew all the right buttons to push and before I had a chance to adjust, I was hooked.

He was the hunter and I was his prey, and like a fragile gazelle caught in the path of a ferocious lion, I succumbed to his demands and his wishes. Instantly, I was initiated into a secret society called the Battered Women's Elite Club.

He was only twenty-five the last time we saw each other, and the awkward ending between us will always remain an imprint on my heart. For a short while, he showed me love and catered to my eagerness to belong, yet I couldn't forget the memories he left behind.

The imprints were near and dear to my heart. Sometimes I wondered if it was because of the way he held me in his arms, or maybe the way he kissed my face when the salty streams of tears ran down my cheeks so many times, wondering what my life would be like without him. Maybe it was because of the many imprints of his fist on the side of my face; even perhaps that time when he smashed my head against the wall or against my car door, when I did not give in to his demands, maybe that is why I can't forget the awkward ending.

I was the only one aware of those imprints, hidden by my dark skin; and remembering thinking how so thrilled I was to be of a very dark hue, helping to conceal my embarrassing secrets.

When things between us were bad—as they often were, I would try to remember the good times rather than the bad times; but no matter how hard I tried, remembering the good times were always overshadowed by the bad times. Those awful times never seemed to go away; they were always effortlessly present. Whenever the small show of a smile appeared on my face, the imprints on my heart would become all too noticeable. It hasn't been easy remembering the good times, no matter how hard I tried to forget the bad times, the memories always drifted into my consciousness.

I would attempt to keep the memories fresh and new, recalling the first time we met; the first time we kissed; the first time we experienced real intimacy, and when he was so very gentle and kind.

I remember when he swept me off my feet, recalling how my heart marched to the beat of his drum. Yet, the awkward ending wouldn't let me forget the imprints he left behind.

Many years after, I wanted to reach out to him, looking for closure and answers for what had gone wrong between us, for what I could have done differently. In my heart, I searched for ways to answer the nagging questions that were already answered, and tried finding ways to make things right again for him. I wanted to give him another chance in the world, yet, somehow, the awkward ending wouldn't allow me to erase the imprints. I repeatedly replayed the scenes in my mind, looking for clues, wondered if I had missed any signs that had been there all along—the signs that had been beaten across my body. The slaps across my face and those I chose to ignore because I didn't want to erase the imprints that were visible on my heart.

I didn't want him to blame me for what had gone wrong in his life or hate me for growing apart from him and maturing; for understanding the difference between my love for him and his possession and control of me. So many times, I wished I could face him without fearing for my life. I longed for a chance to look into his eyes again, to see the stars that once shone so bright. I felt the need to nurture him and to give him a shoulder to cry, but the awkward ending was too much to bear.

The last time we saw each other, he had changed. His eyes filled with tears, and his voice cracked as he spoke my name one last time. He pleaded for me to give him another chance and not to give up on him. He uttered an apology as the police drove him away. Many times, I wanted to write to him, to ask for an explanation for his actions, as if I needed an explanation for what was already so clear.

I was desperate to stay connected even after the awkward ending. I wanted to tell him that I forgave him and for some odd reason, I still felt the need of his validation. I wanted to tell him that his actions were not his fault. Perhaps, it was the company he kept that made him do the things he did. I feared him, loved him, and hated him, all at the same time. For years, my heart bled for him, as well as pitied him, hunted by the thoughts of that near fatal day.

He was almost twenty-five the very last time I saw him, peering at me through the bars of his holding cell, shouting insults at me, and calling me out of my name. He was angry that I had not remained loyal to him, loyal to his abuses. He wanted me to remain obediently under his control, even behind the bars.

He had changed in so many ways, even I could not deny. He no longer was the person I had fallen in love with. Behind those bars was a hardened man, who was crushed and bewildered with anger. He wasn't the same person who left me heartbroken in the parking lot that near fatal day. He had become more solidify in his demeanor—no longer gentle, no longer loving—only full of hatred for me and the rest of the world.

The awkward ending was all that we had left between us. Memories of a vicious past that would forever be imprinted on our hearts and minds.

II

THE EARLY YEARS

It hasn't been easy going back in time. The world, as I knew it all during my young life had always been a place of sadness, shame, and loneliness. My memories at four years of age are as clear today and as transparent as the clear blues of the Caribbean Sea—caught in an ocean of confusion and consumed uncertainties. My memories go so far back as when I found myself in a boarding home, not really understanding or knowing how I had gotten there. It was like traveling in a time zone with no recollection of a previous place. It was like a bad dream that I couldn't wake up from, but with each passing day, the darkness became clearer.

That particular period in my life marked the beginning of my struggle for acceptance and love. I had spent countless years trying to put the pieces together and I rejected the truth of what life had been before this point in my life. As a very young child growing up in Haiti, I was at the mercy of a caretaker whose only intentions were to keep the children in her care beneath the rocks, crushing our young and fragile self-esteem. To this day, I remember Madame Marcel very well, she was well known in her community, her family owned and operated a small orphanage for children whose parents left for America or different parts of the Caribbean in search of a better life—as was my fate. Looking in from the outside, one would say that she and her husband provided a good home and a solid foundation for the children in their care. They owned a large home, and managed a small boutique located on one side of their home. Many of the orphans and pseudo-orphans in their care occupied small rooms on the rear part of their home that was partitioned with makeshift curtains and stackable beds.

Living in the boarding home yielded no happy memories, only resentment, disapproval, and a heavy dose of self-dislike and self-loathing. Madame Marcel was the primary caretaker, although her husband helped occasionally. I remember her strict, regimented ways and how she disciplined us. Those times still make me feel as if sharp objects are piercing my heart. At a very young age, the children in her care were expected to do chores, including cooking, while her own children were allowed to wander around freely. The other children, and I, learned very early on, how to become domesticated. We each were assigned tasks, and were required to perform them with perfection and order. However, for those of us who would mess up occasionally, the punishments were severe. On any given day, Madame Marcel would walk around with her white glove and sometimes her white handkerchief, making sure her furniture was properly polished. If she found any dust at all, that person would be punished accordingly. Sometimes the punishments meant kneeling on raw rice grains or dried beans; and no matter how painful, the child could not move. Other times, the punishment would be to kneel in the corner with our arms extended out for long periods of time.

Madame Marcel's interests were not only in making us good, domesticated children, but also prepare us for our future tasks of serving her family as servants. There was something very crushing about living in that boarding home, a feeling that weighed us down like the dirt pile over a coffin. I think most of us believed that nothing good would come of us, the grimness of our future left our confidence bruised. Feeling completely isolated in a chilling climate with no one to lean on for support, warmth, or comfort, except ourselves.

Looking back at those lonely times at the boarding house, the thoughts of how we were treated made me feel as if we weren't good enough to become anything other than what she had expected. Madame Marcel never let us forgets that her children were better than we could ever be. She was determined to keep us in our place, and in her mind, our place in life was in direct relation to our complexion, which means the darker we were, the more likely we would become servants.

Hearing Madame Marcel utters those all-too-familiar words repeatedly, was like feelings of doom overtaking my senses. The feelings can only described through the eyes of a five-year-old child—all alone with no aspirations. Often I wondered if we were the forgotten and forsaken ones, trying to understand why God would be so cruel as to allow us to be so badly treated.

Overtime, some of us were allowed to help in the boutique, it was there that I began hearing talks about our family—my mother and father. The people who came to the boutique would ask my family name. Some told stories of what they heard or knew of my father and occasionally of my mother, but never with the same recognition that accompanied the mention of my father's name. I began questioning their whereabouts, and really began to notice that they were never present, that I was different from some of the other children. I couldn't remember if I had ever seen them. In my mind, they were of a distant, faded memory. Many questions of their whereabouts haunted me, questions of why they left me. Why they had placed me in that boarding home; and as early as I can remember, I always felt alone, with nowhere to turn; as if the world had forgotten about me.

My circumstance made for relentless and constant teasing by Madame Marcel's children. They teased about my mother, father and family not wanting me, and for as long as I can remember, I believed them. There were never any indications that what the children were saying was untrue. I could not recall anyone ever visiting, no letters asking about my well-being—well, at least not any that I was aware of.

My eyes drifted often to their photographs, my only possession that bore their image; my only link and connection to them, the precious little photograph that I carried with me. Although they had not visit, I recall the occasions when the parcels would come from my mother—and sometimes my father. Most times, Madame Marcel kept the contents of those parcels for her own children. She would say that the items were too pretty for me and her children wore the clothes that were supposed to be for me.

I remember the trinkets, the shoes, flowery dresses, and all the pretty things little girls wanted, yet, sadly, we never experienced the joys of wearing them. I longed to feel those pretty dresses against my skin. I often thought about the care my unfamiliar mother put into selecting those beautiful dresses for me—the chiffon ones; the lacy ones; the pretty, white cotton ones; the blue ones; and the pinks and yellows with matching hair ribbons and socks. How I longed to wear them, and how I longed for them to be mine as they were intended.

All the years of longing to be with my own family was coming to an end, my prayers had been answered! It was the day of the mysterious telegram to Madame Marcel, requesting that she visit the telephone station for a prearranged call. That day was one of the happiest day of my young life, I recalled when she returned from the rendezvous and informing me that I would be leaving her boarding home. I remembered the joy in my heart, and the excitement I felt at the prospect of leaving. I was happy that I would never again have to be a servant. Madame Marcel's wish for me would be unrealized. I became confident, knowing in that moment that my destiny wasn't going to be that of a servant, not what she had wished on me. It was going to be far more than I could ever want.

My excitement was uncontrollable from that day forward. I carried a smile on my face that no one could have taken away. From that day on up to the day I left, I carried a smiled in my heart and on my face, showing all my small pearly teeth. At that moment, I didn't care that some were missing and had not yet grown back. I showed whatever tooth I had left to bear, and although I didn't know all the details of my departure other than the fact I would be leaving—in my mind, I had already left.

The news came with exciting changes, and many happy days followed. For the first time since I lived in that boarding house, Madame Marcel and her family treated me as if I mattered. For the first time, they acted as if they cared. Ironically, they didn't want me to remember how life with them had been, as if treating me kind before I left, would overshadow and erase all the ill treatments of the past. Everyone was excited that my father was coming for me. I didn't want anything to spoil my happy moment. All I cared about was that I was going to a place to be with family.

On the day of my departure, I had been patiently waiting for Father to arrive and take me away from that awful place. I had often wondered what it would be like to come face to face with both my mother and father, but this day all of my wondering would end—at least wondering about my father, that day I saw him for the first time.

I remember studying the sounds of every passing automobile, waiting for the one that would come to a full stop, just for a chance to see if the person stepping out of the automobile was my father. The wait felt like an eternity, but then I heard the sounds of squealing tires on the gravel dirt road that led to the front of the boarding home made me overflow with excitement. I knew in my heart that it had to be him. Even before seeing his face, I trusted in the calmness and peace I felt and the air around me became still as I waited to see the person who would step into the front parlor. I ran to the window for a quick glimpse of the stranger—the man, my father.

This was the moment I had been waiting for, and while peaking through the curtains, I saw him. He looked like his photograph—dark like me. As I listened from the distance, his voice became a familiar sound to my ears. I listened as his footsteps caressed the floor beneath his feet. I listened and waited for the signal—for Madame Marcel to call my name—to enter the parlor, where they had been talking. Finally, she requested our presence. One of the children was sent to find me, but I was there all along, waiting anxiously. I entered the parlor and there he was, sitting with his legs crossed, reclining in the chair! I entered the parlor and greeted the man, my father, with shyness and admiration, and he responded in kind.

"*Bonjour, monsieur,*" I said. (Good afternoon, sir.)

He said my name in calm, soothing voice.

He smiled, and. I smiled back, nodding in agreement.

"*Oui, monsieur,*" I said. (Yes, sir.)

Then he replied, "*C'est moi, ton père.*" (It's me, your father.)

I gazed at him in amazement; it was all I could do to keep my knees from folding under me. Smiling and swinging my body from side to side with joy.

After a brief, uneasy moment between us, my father collected my suitcase—my only possessions—and together we walked out the front door of the boarding home, never looked back, we slowly walked to his automobile with sheer delight.

I prayed that I wasn't dreaming. I prayed that I would never return to Madame Marcel's home and entered my father's automobile and he slowly drove away.

I never looked back to see if anyone was waving good-bye.

I never looked back to see if anyone was sad over our departure.

I never looked back because if I were dreaming, I didn't want to wake up from my dream.

On the long drive to my new home, the two of us spoke very few words, but I felt the warmth of freedom and in that moment of stillness, despite the sounds around us, we both seemed to be at peace with the journey ahead.

After what seemed like a very long drive, we arrived at a small village, it seemed, mysterious. Father pulled up to the large wooden gates and pulled them open, revealing what seemed like a small treasures hidden to the outside world. It was fascinating to see this private village with many homes; the homes sat in a pattern that reminded me of a keyhole. Father drove up the dirt road past some children playing and headed toward a cluster of homes of various sizes and colors. Some had small front porches. On the narrow road, were men and women walking, others standing and sitting, sewing, talking, and laughing.

He drove farther into the village then stopped in front of a small white house with pink framed windows. Father stepped out of the automobile as several people came out of their homes to greet us. I had never met these people, but they already knew my name. They were touching my face smiling. They were as curious to see me, as I was curious to know them. They were talking, laughing, and asking questions that I could not answer.

Perhaps the questions were for my father; perhaps they were just questions floating in the air for anyone to answer. They all seemed to know of me very well, yet I knew nothing of them.

They had never seen me until this day. I never thought there would be so many of them—cousins, great cousins, family friends, and the one person who would have a lasting influence in my life—my older sister Marsha.

Upon meeting her, we had an instant connection, she was nice and nurturing, she welcomed me warmly. She was tall and slim, her eyes were more slanted than mine were, and looking at her and my father, there was no denying that she was his child. She resembled him more than me, almost an exact copy of his image. I was very excited to be with family but most of all with my new sister.

I was also very happy to meet my great auntie, the person who would be my new permanent guardian. My auntie, Madame Joseph was a tall, slender woman of fair complexion with several children of her own, but her husband was deceased. She held my face, and looked at me with admiration and awe. She turned me around from front to back and from side to side again, almost as if she was looking for signs of imperfection, bumps or bruises, as a mother would look at a fallen child with care and concern. After being acquainted with my new families and new friends, we sat down to eat food that was prepared for my arrival. The table was set with lots of good, hearty food—food that I never had at the boarding home. Everyone were talking and laughing, just being happy that I was there, and I was happy to be with them

After the celebration meal was over, I collected my small luggage and followed Madame Joseph, and my sister, to her home, where my sister was also staying and would remain there until our respective mothers returned for us. Being there with Sister Marsha I no longer felt alone, we shared the same outcome because she was also apart from her mother. I was very happy and grateful to be with our father and his family, even if it meant I would have to live with my auntie. I was overwhelmed by how many new families I had met that day, but I wondered where they had been all these years

The day after, I was still very excited about my new outcome; everything was beginning to sink. It was amazing how everything changed so quickly and living a life that I had only dreamed about, when I admired Madame Marcel's children. Our father had requested that a woman be hired to help Auntie Joseph with our care. It was as if I was living a fantasy. It felt great not to be the servant—the one doing all the cleaning—even if it was just for that one day. The woman was to be responsible for cooking and doing whatever else was needed to make our stay comfortable—anything that would minimize the inconvenience to Auntie Joseph.

Madame Joseph seemed as excited to have us in her care, so she wasted no time enrolling us in school. She felt we had not had adequate studies, and she wanted to make up for lost time. Marsha and I were enrolled in the best school that Father could afford. Auntie Joseph saw to it that we wasted no time with child's play, everything was serious and orderly. Everyone knew her to be quite the disciplinarian, with strict morals and values about education. She was always ready to let anyone know that she was a proud Roman Catholic with strong Catholic values. While living in her home, she made certain we read, learned, and recited Bible verses, because she wanted us to become good Catholic girls. Education and religion were always a strong focus in her home.

She never allowed us to miss a day of church, particularly on Sunday, even if it meant going twice. Things were wonderful and we were happy for a while, we felt as if we belonged and we were a part of a real family, the type of family that had been missing in my life.

However, as with anything good, things began to change. Similarities to the boarding home were slowly emerging, although, not nearly as severe. Our father was often away on travel, and Marsha and I began to notice resentment surfacing among family members, jealousy over our father's means. Some of our families apparently felt that Marsha and I was given more than they thought we deserved—a good school and the someone to look after us.

As a young man in Haiti, our father had built a small fortune, valuable only to him, the people around him, and only in his country—nothing that would be recognized elsewhere as a fortune. He owned the homes where most of our families lived in the village. Together with his cousin, they reportedly owned the moderately sized boat that traveled across the sea to the Caribbean importing goods. It was also reported at the time, that they owned many of the autobuses that traveled the provinces of Haiti. Some of the family members disliked them for their success, those members of our family were jealous of what father's children stood to gain if something were to happened to him. Seeing the ugliness of their actions towards Father, caused us to form a very strong bond that was unbreakable. We realized we only had each other.

Father was often too busy with his other responsibilities to care about what others were saying or noticing the changes around him. Even when he was home, which was very rare, his business required all of his time. Being at Auntie Joseph's home, Marsha and I learned that we were not our father's only children. There were many others, with many different mothers and other women wanting the chance to have his children.

There was one in particular among all of the women he was said to have, one of his prospects, we learned was envious of the little bit of time and attention Father paid us. She was particularly jealous of my sister, because as the eldest child, she stood to gain much of what Father possessed or bore the responsibility of having to make decisions no child should have to make, deciding how his possessions would be distributed among his many children.

Her attempt to separate him from us was somewhat successful. She often acted as if she was above us and above him, but she enjoyed the lifestyle he offered her. When they were together, she acted as if she were doing him a favor by being with him, and for whatever reason, he never seemed to notice or saw through her acts. She would often tell him lies about our behavior towards her. She created distance between us, and seemed as if we became outsiders again in our father's home.

Marsha and I gave each other what we each needed. We became friends and confidants. We made each other feel safe, and together—just the two of us—we believed everything would be fine. It was comforting to know that I would never feel alone as long as she was at my side. She had become very special to me, and even though we came together at separate times, and have different mothers, we never made each other feel as if we were half-casts. We gave each other comfort, but the struggle was gaining our father's attention—something he gave very little of from the start. We both wanted very much to please him, to be accepted, and to make him proud. It was my own wish that he knew that I was a good daughter and an obedient child; so that, he would love me as a father loves his child, no matter how many he had.

I believed we both wanted to measure up to his expectations of us, whatever they were. We both wanted to please them all—our father and our family.

III

UNFAMILIAR ENCOUNTER

The news of my mother's visit came as an unexpected surprise, and just as the telegram before, announcing her arrival, like the one that had come from Father nearly two years earlier. Soon my dreams would be complete, the possibility of my mother visiting me never really entered my thoughts as much as before, while living in the boarding home. The feelings of rejection had subsided just a little, because I had my sister with me and we were both in the same situation. Both of our mothers were out of our lives temporarily and suddenly, I did not feel as alone. This was the first time I can recall Mother sending anything since arriving at Auntie's home. Occasionally, when Father returned from his travels, he would tell me that Mother sent her regards, her well wishes and the occasional packages; however, this time, she had sent a written telegram.

I was very excited by the news, the sheer thought of her arrival. In my heart, I've always longed for her, often thinking how different life would have been if we were together. Perhaps she would have been a little more lenient, a little more tolerant of me, and a little more patient and understanding. The days of wondering and imagining about her love for me would soon become my reality, just as when Father visited for me the first and last time at the boarding home. I began hoping that my mother would do the same—remove me from my Auntie's home, not because I no longer liked being there, but because I wanted to be with her, my mother.

Over the time I had been living with Auntie Joseph's and with my father traveling, I learned that Mother was living in the Caribbean even before I was born. I learned that Mother became pregnant with me there, but because she had no family there, had returned to Haiti to have me, but left without me, I've wondered if my life would have been different if I were born there. Now, for the first time since leaving me, she was returning for a visit. I can't ever remember a time when I didn't want her to love me like other mothers loved their children. I longed for her and prayed for her every day. I prayed that God would make me worthy of her love, so much so, that when she saw me, she would want to take me with her.

I had only seen my mother's image from her small photograph that I carried with me; the same one I had while living at the boarding house. That photograph was my only hope that someday we would be reunited. I often looked at her photograph, hoping that she was able to look into my eyes as I looked into hers. I wanted to feel a connection between us, and to feel her heartbeat, just as my heart was beating for her.

I wondered if Mother would like me when we finally met, if she would be as nice and calm as she looked in the photograph. I wondered what it would be like for both of us, after being gone for so long. I was eight years old and I thought about how much I might have changed and grown since she left.

In my little photograph, Mother was so very beautiful.

I admired her beauty, and the peace and tranquility across her face.

I wanted to be so much like her, and be with her in every way.

Many nights before mother arrived, I lay awake, and thought about why she had left. I asked myself questions to which I had no answers. I tried to find all the things she might find imperfect—things that might be wrong with me that I couldn't fix. I worried about the imperfections that may have caused her to leave me and the flaws my eight-year-old eyes couldn't see.

On the morning of Mother's arrival, I prayed she would see past all of my flaws, all of my imperfections. I prayed she would give me the love I hungered for my entire young life and that she would want to reclaim me again.

I hungered to see her beautiful face, just as I had seen it so many times before in her photograph—that beautiful stranger who my mother was. I thought about how she would react when she saw my face, what she would say to me. I wanted to pay special attention to what her eyes would say that her mouth could not speak. Again, I became obsessed with pleasing her, just as I had wanted to please Father. I wanted Mother to like me. My eight-year-old mind raced with many questions I knew I could not ask, but simply had to accept.

The day Mother arrived at my Auntie's front door was unforgettable. The memories are still so vivid. I remember almost the exact detail of what we were doing when she arrived. It was a sunny afternoon, my sister and I were jumping rope with several other children in our village when the taxi drove up the dirt road and came to a stop near us. All the children stopped whatever they were doing—playing marbles, jumping rope, and rolling bike rims down the road, to watch the chauffeur get out of the taxi, held the door open for the stranger who had invaded our village. Like magic, there she was, stepping out of the taxi as if she were royalty, a movie star.

All eyes were in her direction, smiling and embracing her amazing beauty. The chauffeur placed several suitcases on the ground, and a large brown wrapped package. I knew from the way she looked, and the way she was dressed, it had to be her—my mother, this beautiful stranger.

Her present image was true to her photograph. I watched her in admiration; I couldn't believe that she was standing in front of me, that I was seeing her with my very own eyes, looking at her in person. Right then, in the pit of my stomach, I felt her, and in my heart, I loved her.

The encounter was surreal. I remember every detail about that day, and every detail about her—her red lipstick, the radiance of her dark chocolate skin, and the smell of her sweet perfume. I remember the floral patterned blouse she wore with the big red and pink carnation print, the loose sleeves, and the cream-colored flared pants. I remember her shoes, which reminded me of the ones that the *Soul Train* dancers wore when we watched the show on the brown television—with a hangar used for an antenna in my cousin's home.

Mother was even more beautiful than any photograph could ever capture.

While we were standing there impolitely staring at her, she walked up to us, we were still in admiration of her beauty, her flawless looks, and her neatly coiffed hair.

She moved closer and greeted us with an enormous, seemingly wondering smile, as if she did not know who to pick and in our native dialect, she said, "*Bonjour, Enfants.*" (Hello, children.)

We replied, "*Bonjour, Madame.*"

As the rays from the sun that Saturday afternoon shined above, she studied our individual faces, and quickly, out of the group of girls standing there with little to say, she picked me out.

In a questionable voice, she said my name, and I replied, "*Oui, Madame, cest moi.*

I smiled at the sheer delight that she had recognized me from the other girls and knew my name after all those years.

This stranger, looked into my eyes; my curious and questionable eyes. My first thought was to look away, not wanting this stranger to read my thoughts, but then I remember that it was impolite not to look at someone when they were speaking to you, so I forced myself to look at her, searching for answers that her eyes didn't reveal. My years of wondering, all the nights of crying myself to sleep, came down to this very moment. My many questions did not matter anymore. What mattered was that my mother was finally with me. I didn't know how to tell her that I would give my life to be with her forever, and that I didn't want her to leave again now that I had found her.

My mother embraced me, and I embraced her. With nervous hands and uncontrollable energy and eagerness, I hugged my mother with all the strength my little body was able to illustrate. I held her as if my life depended on it, hoping that this day would be the start of a new connection and a new beginning between us.

Mother's visit brought me so much happiness. I was comforted knowing that she next to me, and being so close to her was all that needed. I thought that nothing could have taken that moment away. During her visit, she stayed with family, but would visit me as often as she was able to, but no sooner had she assured me that everything would be t fine, the rumors began to spread and people began talking.

The rumors were about her intentions and the real reason behind her visit, soon after she arrived, people were speculating that her visit had nothing to do with her taking me back to the Caribbean when she got ready to leave. Rather, her visit was really to take another child back with her who wasn't her own—the daughter of her new husband and it was just convenient for her to handle seeing me and taking this other girl all in one trip. I tried ignoring the rumors. There wasn't anything that would make me believe that my mother would abandon me again now that she had found me.

The many weeks of harmony in my heart, had become torments. The rumors were true, my mother was taking this other girl with her to the Caribbean—the girl I dubbed the faceless girl—and leave me once again. I felt disappointed, bewildered and all the emotions that can be used to describe complete isolation and abandonment. I felt like a complete failure—an unwanted and unlikeable failure, because whatever my mother's plans were, did not include me. I was not going to be part of her happy family. I was devastated, and the reality of my destroyed wish hit me like a ton of bricks. Mother had made her decision, her choice but I was not her choice. Whatever her reasoning, timing, money issues, I could not understand why she would leave me again and at that moment I felt as though I would never be with her again.

# IV

STRANGE MEDICINE

As the time approached for Mother to leave, I was becoming accepting of the fact that I would have to wait my turn to be with her. Although the visits continued, they became less frequent and were not as joyous as they had been previously. The day before she was to return to the Caribbean, we shared one last unforgettable day together—only the two of us. I thought Mother was trying to make up for having to leave me. I felt it was her way of sharing her time between the faceless girl and me. She had planned this special trip to the mountains, to pray to the saints for protection while she was away, almost like a pilgrimage.

Our day started with a visit to the market; Mother had to buy things she needed for our trip to the mountain. We had to walk on a the dirt road and the hot morning sun blazing down on us, I remember us rushing to get to the roadside and fortunately we arrived on the roadside in time to board an autobus to the hillsides of the province. The autobus was filled to the brim, people stood shoulder to shoulder, sitting on top of the bus, standing on the bumpers, filling any space that was left, no matter how small.

When we arrived at our destination, the autobus let us off on a hilly road, where an elderly woman awaited our arrival. She led the way and we followed. Together, the three of us carefully climbed a small hill. The elderly woman led us to a small village hidden behind the trees. The small shacks were made from banana leaves with aluminum covers lined the hillside. The atmosphere was calming and peaceful after our long journey, the birds were flying above us and the sun was cascading through the trees. The elderly woman led us to one of the shacks, where an older man waited. He greeted us with extended hand and Mother responded in kind. He invited us into his home and we entered slowly and consciously.

Inside the small, aluminum covered shack were many strange things I had not seen before, at least not in the manner they were being presented. I was both amazed and scared. Some of the things seemed unnatural; I studied every inch of the shack, wondering what those things were doing there, what they were used for, because they did not seem to have any use or value. I wondered what type of person he was and why he was living among all those dead things.

I recall his complexion being of clay like color—almost matching the reddish dirt floor beneath our feet's. His hair was thin and gray; his body, frail and thin. Even though my mother was within my reach, I was afraid of the things around us. He asked Mother about her reason for visiting. She explained that she had knowledge of someone wanting to harm me, and that she wanted to make sure no harm came to me while she was away.

The old man was an herb doctor, and he was going to make everything better for Mother and me.

They continued their conversation, and my mind was in a stupor. I was transfixed on the strange objects, especially the skulls—human and animal skulls were hanging in the corners of the shack. To anyone one else, it would appear that he had robbed the nearest graves for their remains—small skulls as well as dead animals in jars lined the walls.

Sensing my fear, Mother explained to me that our visit to the voodoo priest was for my own safety and protection. She stooped down to put money on a round, straw tray with cards that were resting on the floor.

As the old man picked up the cards and began shuffling them, he mumbled words and changed to a low voice. Next, he sipped from a brown bottle that was on the floor next to his feet. He spat on the floor, and continued his chanting.

He tied a red scarf around his head and then set alight some cotton mesh lying on a white porcelain plate next to numerous framed portraits of Catholic saints.

He asked Mother to separate the cards into two parts as he continued chanting.

He picked up one of the two stacks of cards and began to turn each one face up on the straw tray. Every card was different from the other; each had a different image—snakes, skeletons, animals—and each symbolizing a different outcome. With each card, he revealed the story he saw table to identify from the images, and told Mother what each card represented about me and about her. One of the reasons for Mother's visit was also to see about having other children since she was now married. She learned that something or someone was trying to keep her from getting pregnant, and he was to break the spell.

Mother and I listened intently to him, but I did not understand everything that he was saying. Some of the cards revealed good harmless stories with good outcome, whereas others were not as pleasant. He described fate of a positive nature, plus violence and death.

After the card-reading ritual, the elderly man instructed Mother and me to prepare for a "bush bath." I didn't understand why we had to take a bath again so soon, I was worried about taking off my clothes in front of this strange, old man. With great resistance on my part, we stripped down to our underpants in front and stood in a large aluminum tub as he mixed his concoction of unexplainable things. Mother had purchased the requested items that morning—fresh goat's milk, holy water, *cerasee* bush plant, champagne, and copper pennies from her handbag, plus orange peels and lemongrass, which he added. He poured the mixture over our heads and chanted. I felt so cold, even though a hot summer breeze swept around the mountain, the chills raced across my frame as he poured the mixture and chanted.

The ritual seemed to last for an eternity, and after it was all over, I felt remarkably strange.

Upon returning to my Auntie's home, I wondered and contemplated what I would tell my sister when she asked about my day. Perhaps she would smell the strange odor that lingered in my hair and clothes. What would I say to my auntie when she questioned the makeshift bandage that covered the small cut at the top of my right arm that my dress sleeves could not cover, and as we made our way back to my father's village, Mother cautioned me not to tell anyone about our day.

As I had expected, everyone wanted to know exactly where we had gone. They wanted details, but so much happened that day, I did not want to speak about any of it. Even though I said very little, they had their own suspicions. Because it was a special day between Mother and me, I wanted the day to be a secret I shared only with her. They called me unpleasant names when I refused to say, and for days afterward, those who were once close to me—my sister Marsha became somewhat withdrawn from me and me with her. I felt she sided with the others and briefly left me to take up for myself. I never really blamed her; I just had to give her time. I thought if I did not get close to them again, they wouldn't ask me to speak of the day with my mother.

I was afraid that Mother would be angry with me for telling about our special trip. Yet, I was afraid that my Auntie would be angry with me for not telling her, but she already had her suspicions. Auntie Joseph began praying loudly, and recited verses from the Bible, while praying, she asked god to forgive Mother and me for looking to the other side for answers. I was afraid of picking sides, and felt that I would be betraying my mother while disobeying my Auntie, the person who had been caring for me.

After Mother left for the Caribbean with the faceless girl, Auntie and my older cousins grilled me about our trip, so much so that I eventually broke down and told them everything. I was afraid of what they might do to me. A part of me felt betrayed by my mother, angry at her for not protecting me and for putting me in a awkward position with my Auntie and the rest of my family. Unknowingly, Mother left me alone to handle the inquisition. I decided to tell them everything, to restore the peacefulness I once share with my Auntie and family before Mother's arrival.

I answered all of their questions. Telling my Auntie about the jars filled with lizards and other creatures. I told her about the skulls hanging in the corners, and the dead snakes floating in clear liquid in bottles that rested on a shelf made of bricks and wobbly wood.

I told her about the special bath the man had given Mother and me, and how we stood in the metal tub waiting for him to pour the mixture over our heads. I described the ingredients and told her of the things I remembered—the holy water, the *cerasee* bush plant, the bottle of champagne, and the milk—and about the special small cut that he had made after the bath on my right arm with the razor. The small cut was to represent my guardian—something small no one would question—but they did.

I showed Auntie the small cut and even though it wasn't very big, it still made me cry.

I told her about how I was scared when he cut me, how I was afraid of the razor he used.

I spoke of the things I saw as if my life depended on it. I told my auntie how the special bath was to protect mother and me from bad things, bad spirits, and people who wanted to do us harm. I told her that after the bath, we dressed and sat around the tray table again for another card reading. This time, though, he shuffled the cards and arranged them in a circle. He tied two satin scarves around his waist—one black and one blue.

I told her how his voice changed when he spoke. I explained how he drank from the brown bottle with the three stars and sprayed the liquid from his mouth on each side of him on the dirt floor. I told her that he burned the cotton mesh that had been soaked in oil.

"He spoke in his womanly voice, and asked Mother and me to drink from the brown bottle and spat the liquid on the ground as he had done, an offering to our dead ancestors, to ask for their protection."

I told her how the liquid in the bottle burned my mouth and how after we drank from the bottle; he went outside the tin-covered shack. Pouring the liquid by the door and on each corner of the shack, as a small offering to all the deceased, so that together their spirit of all the ancestors so they may protect us against harmful spirits.

He spoke in a woman's voice.

The three of us were seated on a straw mat. Mother and I sat close together and he on the other side of us with the large tray between us. He shuffled the cards, spread them on the tray, and spoke in a woman's deep voice—a voice that didn't match the male figure sitting in front of us.

He picked up the first card and explained to Mother, in a woman's voice, what the symbols on the card told him. He then began reading card after card. Mother proceeded to place more money on the straw tray across from him.

"He instructed Mother to repeat the ceremonial chants after him," I told Auntie. "He told her what to do, and she placed the rest of the money on the tray. As he moved slowly and chanted, his voice returned to a typical male voice."

"Afterward," I added, "he asked Mother if the spiritual woman who spoke through him had spoken to her and told her what she needed to do. This was my very first experience with a voodoo priest. He gave us another drink from a different bottle—the bottle with the bush plants inside—and a cup of milk with a green lizard inside. He said the mixture would protect us from any poison. Without questioning him, Mother and I drank from the bottle and of the milk concoction, and his job was done."

After telling my auntie about our trip, she insisted that I get on my knees and pray to God for forgiveness of my sins and for my darkened soul. I prayed longer than I had any other night before.

Everyone in our village knew where Mother and I had been. The other children didn't want to play with me anymore, and for the first time since being together, my sister and I were distant. The way Auntie spoke of Mother and me made others keep their distance. The most painful thing for me was that my mother had left me—the person who had been with me through this experience together was now avoiding me. I felt isolated and burdened. I felt confused about everything. I wondered why, if this thing was supposed to protect me, why was it that people were staying away from me. I wondered why everyone thought there was something wrong with me.

The day following Mother's departure, Auntie spared no time getting my sister and me to church so that the white priest at our church would cast out what she thought were demon spells on my body and mind, when we entered the empty church, we sat in the front pew as Auntie recounted my story to the priest. Afterward, he said a prayer, burned some scented hazy thing around us (which I later learned were incents), and blessed us with holy water. After he finished with his prayers and reading from the bible, he pronounced me as one of God's children again. He sent us on our way with a small bottle of holy water to bless our home.

I thought of my mother leaving truly devastated me. I felt angry that she had left me behind, and I felt shame. What was most hurtful was that someone else, another girl—the faceless girl had taken my place in her life. My heart was broken. I saw myself as an unwanted child. Those feelings shaped the rest of my life.

Throughout the eight years of life, I always wanted to earn her love and acceptance. The reality of not being—and feeling wanted by my mother, who was already very distant, crushed my hopes. She did not choose me, and that was an unbearable truth to bear. Her decision was clear to everyone and although that may not been her intentions, there was no other way to rationalize the facts. Everyone said she favored her new husband's daughter. I wondered if she even loved me at all, because her actions suggested otherwise. All I wanted was her love; nothing Mother could have said to me at that point would have made me feel any better about her decision. (I later learned that the faceless girl's mother had died while they lived in Haiti, and because her father was living somewhere else in the Caribbean at the time, she had been taken in by an uncle.) However, when her father married my mother, it was time for her to reunite with him.

I was very, very sad for a long time after Mother left, but I refused to believe that my own mother would forsake me. I refused to believe what everyone said about me and about her. I wanted to believe that she would come back for me, just as she had promised. I didn't want to accept that my own mother had chosen another child over me—someone who wasn't her own flesh and blood.

Even after she was long gone, it was hard to accept what was very clear, obvious, and unchanged. I kept going over the events in my mind, thinking about the rumors and hoping that, even if they were true, she would take us both—me and the faceless girl—but the timing wasn't right.

V

LOSING A FRIEND

Several months after Mother's departure, another confusing chapter in my life presented itself—the death of my young friend, Yannic. Her death was sudden and unexpected. It was hard to believe that she was gone and would not be return. I remember that she was very funny and kind; she was as much as a sister to me as was Marsha. She was a kind and funny girl, our friendship evolved innocently overtime while shooting marbles on our spare time, although short lived, our friendship developed shortly after I began living with

Auntie Joseph, when we first saw each other. Moments of laughter punctuated our time together. She was very special in my life; she was so full of spirit, and would always bring a smile to my face when things seemed gloomy. Both of her parents had died when she was very young, and she was placed in the home of a family member, who lived in our village and walked with a leg brace.

From the time Yannic arrived, she was responsible for everything in her home. She never seemed to mind the responsibilities, or that she didn't get much rest. She was constantly working—completing an enormous list of daily chores. How she was in her home reminded me of when I lived in the boarding home, except that she was always happier.

Yannic had so much joy and love in her little body, and those feelings were contagious. I admired the endless smiles on her face, her dark chocolate skin, and her thick wavy hair. I admired how she did everything with such pride and always in a rush. She appreciated that her aunt had given her a chance to have a family again. She always had a kind word to say about the other children in our village and one of the many things we enjoyed doing was playing in the fields behind her home. We enjoyed pretending we were somewhere other than our village—other than Haiti. We wanted to be like the white children we saw on my cousin's television. We ran in the fields and played hide-and-seek until someone came looking for us or we heard our names called.

Other times we enjoyed going to the small, muddy creek to pick leeches for her aunt's bad leg. The leeches' were to remove the contaminated blood that caused her so much pain, while other people in the village also used them for treatment on their backs.

On our way to the creek, we would talked about everything—things that made sense only to us. Our conversations were full of color, dreams, fantasies, and excitement. I liked walking with her. I was mesmerized by her bravery every time she collected those leeches and placed them in small jars. She had a way with collecting them without being bitten. Sometimes, she would chase me around, trying to place one of those leeches on my leg because she knew how much I was afraid and hated them. I remember all the fun times we shared together.

I missed her so much; she lived bravely up to the day she died. When the news came about her sudden death, everyone was surprised.

Her untiring spirit was engaging, always reminding me of someone who had lived on this hearth before. She made me feel comfortable being around her; she was like an old soul in a child's body—so full of wisdom beyond her youthful years.

I remembered us playing together the days before she died; our conversations about my mother's departure, about the dead of her own parents, and how it made her feel. She consoled me, helping me understand and appreciate that my own parents were both alive, regardless of how far they were. We spoke about how much we would miss each other when the day came for me to leave Haiti. I remember the good times we shared, playing in the summer rain, the mudslides that would wash us down the village during heavy rain falls, washing away anything standing in its way. Whenever there was heavy rain, we would run to the top of the small hill and let the rain washed us down as if we were on a slide.

I remembered us shooting marbles together and how she often beat me at it. She taught me a few tricks to strike the marbles out of the circle when we played against the other children. I remembered us sitting around daydreaming in my Auntie's backyard beneath the big tree covered with loffa gourd vines. We enjoyed sitting together in the dark in my cousin's backyard, watching his homemade silent karate cinemas while roasting corn over an open fire, as the adults made up stories about karate and the lady mermaid in the river.

The news of my friend's death was cutting, because we had played together the night before and she was happy and laughing. She did not appear sick, and if she had been, I am almost certain she would have told me. The news traveled from one home to another in our village early that morning, and it surprised everyone who had heard of it. No one could make sense of my friend's sudden departure. No one could understand what could have taken her life overnight. Some speculated that spells were the culprit; others thought that maybe her soul had been given for labor—to work the sugar cane fields. Still others thought she must be living among the zombies in the mountains.

Reliving that day still brings back surreal memories. She reportedly died in her sleep. I was sad that I never had a chance to say good-bye to my friend. I wondered how someone so young, with no signs of illness, had been taken so quickly. Her death left me with many questions—unspoken and unanswered.

Yannic's body was sent to the province for burial where she would lay to rest next to her mother and father. My memories of her remained as I saw her last—the night before—happy, smiling, and full of joy and laughter. I recalled that she was wearing her favorite print dress. I remembered her beautiful spirit and that I never said good-bye to my friend. I remember that there had been a great deal of sadness in my life— now including the loss of my dearest friend—and that I had not yet moved beyond my feelings of loss and disloyalty after my mother left. I was still disillusioned and confused by all the events of the past months. I felt broken and despondent.

VI

THE JOURNEY AHEAD

I was angry with God for being so cruel, and for taking my friend away so early. I struggled to understand all the things that were going wrong. I wanted to understand why Mother sacrificed me for the sake of another child. My entire existence was built on hopes of one day living that better life. I wanted so much to be part of Mother's life and part of her new family. I wanted acceptance and love just as she had freely and openly accepted and loved her husband's daughter.

I mourned for both of them, Mother and my friend; my family couldn't understand why I would cry to be with someone who apparently didn't want me. I resorted to remembering how things were before Mother had visited, trying to accept what was in front of me. I had heard the continuous gossiping, the rumors, and each version varied from one person to the next, but what they said did not matter anymore.

I remembered Mother telling me how the faceless girl needed to be with her father because of her own mother's death, I listened to all the reasons why she couldn't take me; why, maybe in her mind she may have thought that the faceless girl was more deserving than I. I thought about my desire to be with her. I needed her in ways I couldn't express. I detested the faceless girl and her father before I even met them. I felt they had ruined my chances with my mother. She left me with the promise that she would return for me soon. I held to that promise because it was all I had. Months after Mother's departure, I continued my silent cries, while holding on to her promise that she would see me again someday soon.

Time passed on and the summer rains came and left. Yet, I kept watch for that mysterious taxi to return just as it had before. I wanted it to drive up the dirt road again, but there was no such taxi. Many days, I looked out the windows, hoping Mother would be there at the front door, but that day never came. Months passed since she promised me she would return for me and we would be together.

Over time, the tears from my tears dried up, but my heart cried with sorrow every day, still trying to understand why Mother had not returned, why I wasn't the chosen one.

Every so often, I would think about the faceless girl. I thought about how special she must have been, and how special she must have felt when my mother chose her over me. Thinking how lucky she must have been to win my mother's heart.

With each passing day, though, I began to feel laughter in my heart again because I held on to the belief and hope that the day would come for me to leave Haiti. The realization of my dream to see my mother again came one day by way of my father. It was after returning from one of his many voyages to the Caribbean. He announced to the family that my sister and I would be leaving with him on his next journey! The only other times I remember being happy was when his telegram arrived at the boarding house announcing his plans to visit, and when I learned of my mother's visit.

My sister and I were as excited as anything. We were overcome with joy at the prospect of traveling and leaving our homeland for a better life in the Caribbean. I felt hope again about seeing my mother. The thoughts of her had never left my heart, and the possibility of seeing her one day had not faded. Even when I thought she might have forgotten her promise, I still didn't give up hope.

My father's announcement brought back the memories, the tears, and the sadness that I was hiding. I was filled with a sense of gratitude to my father for once again rescuing me and my sister as he did when we were at the boarding home, and for trying to reunite Mother and me.

It had been months since the announcement, and the plans for our voyage were forging ahead. Everyone was excited about the opportunities that the journey would afford us. Marsha and I were happy about our new adventure. Although I didn't want to seem ungrateful, when I thought about how Marsha and I were traveling, I felt jealous of the faceless girl. We had often heard of the teasing and taunting of other people who had traveled in the same manner we were to travel--in the banana boat, as stowaways.

The thought was crushing, because my father was a man of means and. I couldn't understand why my sister Marsha and I could not travel by airplane as Mother and the faceless girl had done. It took time for me to I understood the reason, that we didn't have the proper documentations. My father believed the authorities wouldn't allow us to travel or would restrict his travel if they thought that we would not return to Haiti on a travel visa--if they would even grant one. He didn't want to take any chances, so our best option was to travel as Father had arranged.

The faceless girl haunted my every thought—how she had been allowed to travel by airplane, why our circumstances were different. Perhaps she had come from a privileged family. Maybe she was fair and pretty. I'd imagine that her family were very important at one time in society and had established good ties with others to grant them the passage she need. Maybe one day her luck would be mine.

VII

STOWAWAY

For us to travel in the timeframe Father had planned, we had to go as stowaways like the cargo on his boat. Part of me wanted the same privileges as the faceless girl who had taken my place in my mother's heart. I was jealous of her special treatment. I wanted to be validated as being as worthy as she. Therefore, our only chance of ever leaving Haiti was to be smuggled out.

The closer we got to the day of our journey, the more excited I became. My sister and I were happy that for the first time, we would see a new place, and experience a different life. We had heard so many wonderful stories about the Caribbean from the people who had traveled there, and soon we would see it for ourselves. The Caribbean, we were told, were home to people of great means. They were said to have big beautiful homes furnished for kings and queens, big automobiles, and celebrations with music and dancing that lasted from Friday to Sunday. We heard rumors that people frequently found money on the pavement.

We wanted to see all of it for ourselves and couldn't wait to experience those wonderful dreams.

The plan was in motion. We bid farewell to our families and friends one last time and left with our father for his home—which neither my sister nor I knew existed until this day—in the province, where we were scheduled to board the boat. We climbed aboard one of the many buses my father owned. When we arrived at his house, we were fascinated with its grandeur. It was hidden behind scattered trees and mountains against an ocean backdrop.

Marsha and I were amazed that our father owned a home of such magnitude, though we were aware that he owned the homes in our village, this was the largest and most beautiful of them all. It was decorated with special things from his travels—modern amenities we only saw on television. With each step, we explored every corner of his large home. The most beautiful sight ever was the sunset coupled with the blue of the ocean—like a perfect picture on a sunlit afternoon. In the distance, I could see my father's large boat floating in the vast ocean where people fished for the fresh catch of the day.

It was the first time we had seen his large boat, even though we had heard about it from others. Seeing it up close was even better than anyone had described! There was the boat that would take us across the ocean to a much better life, and upon seeing that boat, I decided that being a "banana boat" person would probably not so bad after all.

I was in paradise. I couldn't think of anything else other than our journey ahead, and I was the happiest I had been in a long time—since Mother had arrived. As we awaited our departure, I daydreamed about my new life, and a new paradise. I was at peace with myself, embracing the harmony of the nature, and enjoying the tranquility I felt as I watched the ripples of the waves hit my skin. I daydreamed about my new and happy life with Mother who awaited me.

My sister and I occupied ourselves by watching the porters travel back and forth across the ramp, loading the boat with crops, barrels, and merchandise. It was exciting to feel part of something so adventurous. The magnitude of my father's influence was clear—the grand boat, the workers who answered to him and his home. His life in this hidden, quiet treasure, and peaceful place revealed a father we had not known.

Father was always very secretive about his life, the many women, and the many children we were told that he had. He was a distant man with little attachment to anyone; even the actual day and month of his birth remained a guessing game. Although we knew he loved us, he didn't express his affection. It was just assumed we would know how he felt. My father wasn't comfortable with vulnerability. We weren't especially close, the relationship was that of a provider, although we sensed that he was proud of us, but that remained to be seen. Living in our father's home for those short weeks made it clear what little Marsha and I knew of the man and he planned on keeping it as such.

During our short stay, we tried our best to remain out of his way while he conducted business. The cooks made sure that we were properly fed and cared for. Each morning after breakfast, Marsha and I would head to the beach to watch the fishermen in their small canoes casting their nets for the day's catch. We would skip over the ocean waves in the early morning sun, playing and feeling free, waiting for the day when we would finally leave on our journey.

The night before our voyage, one of Father's workers tried to hurt me. Marsha and I had been playing until sunset, when it was time for us to go inside, Marsha went in, but I decided that I would play a little bit longer. I was captivated by the sun looming over the ocean's surface, and the feel of the sand beneath my feet; knowing that by morning we would be gone. I was tossing stones at the waves, watching the men and women making their way home from fishing. As soon as it was getting, I began heading toward the house, several feet's away. The porter saw me as I was going into the house and ask that I help him gather some charcoal for the cook inside at the nearby shack to take with me, since he was not allowed inside Father's home.

Innocently, I followed him into the shack where the charcoals were kept. I was so lost in thought about leaving in the morning that it hadn't occurred to me to stay outside the shack while he gathered the charcoal, as we entered the shack; he closed the door, secured the latch, and reached for me. He tried to force me on the ground.

We tussled, and I pushed his hands away from my body. Trying to get away from him, he tried covering my mouth with one of his hand, but I bit his fingers and managed to break free from his hold. He grabbed hold of my arms, pulled me back, and tried pushing me down on top of the hay pile in one of the corner. He tried ruthlessly to put his hand up under my dress, but I kicked him. I scrambled to my feet and ran from the shack. As I ran toward the house, I noticed that my dress was torn and dirty with black dust from the charcoal. I was so shaken, but I was more concerned about my dress. I didn't know how I was going to explain to my father what had happened.

I sat down just behind Father's home contemplating my fate, how I would explain why my dress was torn and dirty. Father was coming out the back door to look for me. It was fully dark and passed the time that I should be outside; I expected father would be angry with me. He saw me sitting in the dark, shaken and whimpering, but his concerns were more about disobeying him, not being inside the home where I was expected to be. Father demanded to know why I had not gone inside with my sister. I tried explaining, but he would not listen, He removed his belt and began beating me. He never gave me a chance to explain, that was the first only time Father had ever hit me. I never told anyone what really happened that night before we left Haiti—not even my sister.

At dawn, we were awakened to begin our journey, I was already missing what I came to appreciate about my country—how proud we were as a people, how generous most of us were with others, our spirit, and all that was good—the food and the simplicity of life itself. Nevertheless, I wouldn't forget the unpleasant circumstances.

For the last time, Marsha and I appreciated the morning dew and the sun peeking over the horizon, feeling the moist, soothing mountain air and the brisk wind against our skin. The waves were quietly swaying in a melodic beat against the rocks. We knew our home would be no more. With nervous energy and tired eyes, we awaited the journey ahead.

My father, Marsha and I, made our way in the small fishing boat. We slowly drifted toward the large boat whose cargo had already been packed the afternoon before. We paddled quietly to blend in with the natural sound of the waves. We tried avoiding attention to our small craft, while Marsha and I were covered with a large burlap sack, we reached the boat unnoticed and undetected.

Like thieves in the night, we made our escape. Once on board the larger boat, the crew quickly ushered Marsha and I below deck. To have been discovered or captured by the authorities would have meant imprisonment for my father or perhaps even death, since he didn't have permission for my sister and me to travel. As stowaways, we hid inside makeshift boxes under sacks of grain, plantains, and bananas.

The boxes were large enough for one squatting adult, but my sister and I shared one. We were cramped into a sitting fetal-like position, with barely any room to move an elbow. We managed to put our arms around each other and quietly cuddled until we were given the signal to roam freely. Others were already on board—some elderly women risking the remainder of their lives for a chance to be free and gain worldly possessions in the Caribbean.

While inside that box, our hearts raced with fear, worrying that the authorities might check below deck one more time before they gave the captain permission to leave; wondering if we would be free from deaths gate in our own land or cast into the sea.

Finally the boat was moving, headed toward freedom. The time in that cramped box seemed like an eternity, and then we heard movement, the captain had given the order for us to move about below deck, but no sooner had we been at sea, panic began to set in because of the reported leaks. Cracks that had not been detected or repaired were now apparent as the ocean water beat against the boat. Water was slowly seeping in, but eventually things were back in order.

We lost total track of time and before we knew it, it was night. There was lots of noise, which was coming from the bottom of the boat, the knocking sound from the engine and the people moving about, still trying to remove any water coming into the boat with buckets and cans, or whatever was within their reach. The smell of the tar they used to repair the cracks on the metal was nauseating.

Marsha and I were happy to finally be allowed go on the top deck, amazed at the darkness, the fresh ocean air and now the seemingly small boat in this vast ocean was lit only by the small lamps and the candles we carried. We were amazed at the vastness of the ocean and at the darkness that covered the sky—a blanket of shadows like no other. We could only see the stars, and the denseness of the night felt oppressive. We feared something sinister was lurking. The first night on the boat felt strange. There were moments of absolute calmness other times; the boat took a beating from the roaring sea. The openness of that mighty ocean made us quiver, and tested our strength and composure.

Nights turned into days, and days into nights. After days of calmness and suddenly the calmness was no more. A roaring thunder and storm broke the silence. Everyone was terrified of the sudden rage of the sea. The wind and waves were thrusting against the boat with fierce intensity, rocking it from side to side, beating it violently. The boat swayed and dipped. Water and rain poured into the boat, Father, the captain, and the other men and women on board rushed to remove the water as quickly as it was coming in.

The captain sent us below deck again, so that we wouldn't fall overboard. We did not have the strength to withstand the boat's thrusting motion. The journey was torturous; neither my sister nor I had ever been on an extended voyage, much less on a boat as big as this one and in a storm as angry as this one. The storm was certainly not like the heavy rainfalls that produced the mudslides we enjoyed playing in. This was different and very frightening. I clutched onto my sister, and held her tightly for comfort until we dozed asleep.

By morning, the sea was calm again, as if the storm had never happened. Above the now peaceful sea, birds flew and the sun's rays were bright.

I can't recall how many days we were at sea—the days and nights seemed to merge into one, but as we were neared our destination, we were instructed to remain hidden below deck until someone told us that it was safe to come out again and meet our family and friends who were awaiting our arrival.

When we finally arrived, everyone cried out, *"Merci, Jésus, Mon Dieu!"* (Thank you, Jesus, my God!)

We were joyful that we had reached our destination without any casualties. No one had jumped to his or her death out of fear of captivity. We were free.

VIII

DEFINING MOMENT

Our dangerous and exciting journey had come to an end, and the moment I had been waiting for—the day I would face my mother again—was imminent. Almost nearly two year earlier, was after Mother's unforgettable visit, it was unimaginable that I would be here waiting to look into my mother's eyes again, looking for the connection we had nearly ten years ago.

As with the other onlookers, my mother was in the crowd of people waiting at the gate. My father accompanied us off the boat. Mother was searching the crowd of people for familiar faces, and I was searching for her familiar face. I recognized her from a distance—her portrait had never left my thoughts. The image of her face had never faded from my dreams. Seeing her again in person was all that my heart desired. I was pleased to see her waiting for my arrival after what had seemed like a lifetime. Her face had not changed much, but something else about her was different. Her belly was big and round.

More than two years had passed since our last encounter, but this time she was glowing. She looked more radiant than I had remembered. She was more beautiful than the day she visited me in Haiti. Mother was accompanied by a portly, slightly balding man with wavy hair. A girl about my age and height accompanied them as well. Immediately, I knew that she was the faceless girl who had haunted my dreams—my replacement—his daughter, the chosen one.

Also next to us were two other women. One woman was introduced as my *grandmère* and the other woman we had met in Haiti years earlier, with my brothers, when they visited father. Mother embraced me, but this time I was more cautious than before, she looked at me, and turned me around to see if I was still the same child. She held my face and gently shifted it from side to side, as if looking for signs of change, and signs of maturity. After her thorough inspection, she introduced us—my father, sister, and me, to the man and the girl standing next to us. My father stood at our side and exchanged pleasantries while my sister and I smiled and gazed at the girl.

I studied the girl's face and posture. I didn't need an introduction. I knew instantly who she was, although I had not seen her face until now. Since the day Mother had left with her, a vision of the girl had haunted my thoughts. I imagined how her beauty would compare to mine. I wondered if she was like me in any way. At that moment, as she stood in my presence, I didn't know what to say. I wanted to scream at her in a jealous rage. I loathed her for taking my place. I wanted to hurt her feelings the way my feelings had been hurt and my heart had been broken. However, I couldn't find the courage to hate her because she was like me.

We stood together in front of my mother, and I felt sorry for the faceless girl, as I had felt for myself. I felt sorry that she had lost her own mother so suddenly, and I imagined she understood how my heart was hurting.

Looking at the faceless girl next to me for the first time, I felt we shared something similar. We were confused children living in an adult controlled world that we didn't understand. We were victims of circumstance.

Mother smiled and asked about my journey and the conditions of our travel. I was at a loss for what to say except that all went well. Then it was *his* turn to speak.

"*Comment vas tu?*" the portly man asked, as if we were long lost friends. ("How are you?")

Politely I replied, "*Très bien, merci, monsieur.*" ("Fine, thank you, sir.")

There wasn't much else to say. I was nervous about meeting Mother and her new family; I didn't want my fears to show. This was a great day of my reunion with my mother. I was just glad to be there.

After several exchanges, it was time to say good-bye to Father and my *grandmère*. But worse of all I had to said good-bye to my sister, who would be living with *grandmère* and Father. It was very hard saying good-bye to Marsha, the one person who had been my protector, my best friend, and like a mother to me. I was grateful that our lives had come together at the boarding house. I was happy that our paths had crossed. Although I was happy to see my mother, I didn't want my sister to leave. My sister was familiar and safe.

Since I had known my sister, she had been everything to me; she taught me most of all how to be strong. I couldn't imagine living in this new place without her by my side. Yet, I knew this was how it was going to be, and already my life seemed lonely and empty without her.

I embraced her for a lifetime just in case we didn't see each other again. We promised to write each other, and to keep in touch. I missed her the moment we turned to go our separate way. I knew that our lives would never be as they had been. I prayed she would be in a better place with my *grandmère* and father. I prayed that I would be in a good place with my mother and her new family.

On the drive to their home in the automobile he drove, Mother sat next to the portly man's in the front seat and I sat behind them, next to my rival. He drove up to a wide house that was painted a yellowish color. Outside their home were automobiles and a few people talking. When the automobile came to a stop, the portly man stepped out and unloaded my small suitcase, and we walked into the home. The layout of the home reminded me so much of the homes in Haiti. Inside, people were waiting to see me. The introductions began as I nervously made my way through the small house.

I was surrounded by lots of strangers—their friends and family, I felt overwhelmed; some pulled and tugged at me, conveying their excitement about seeing me. Moving from one person to the next, introducing myself to them. People I didn't even know embraced me and in a corner of the house people sat at a table playing cards. The room was filled with smoke. On the table were red chips, money, cards, and dominos. Most of the people were shouting, and swearing at each other for having lost their money, but when one game was over, another would start, and the disagreements continued. Shortly after arriving, mother joined the games and I was left with the faceless girl for guidance. I followed her around, watching her every move, always right behind her. Then she turned the corridor and went into the room we would share.

The room was large, with a bunk bed against the wall next to a big window with lacy curtains. The walls were pink and the floor was white ceramic. There was a chest for my clothes on the other side of the room. After careful observation, I placed my suitcase on the foot of the bed and the girl showed me the bunk that would be mine. It was the bottom one, which had already been decided. I recalled sitting in the room with her. I gazed at the walls, and didn't know what to do or say. I didn't understand her language and I wasn't sure how much of my language she remembered. For a while, we stared at each other, and we stared at the floor in silence with our thoughts. I remember thinking she was very pretty, sun-kissed brown hair to match her skin and brown eyes.

I remember thinking how similar we were, but so very different. She was so much prettier and so much better than I could ever hope to be.

It had been several months since arriving, yet I still felt like an intruder—an outsider. The newness and excitement of being in a new country had quickly waned. The celebration had ended as quickly as it had begun. Overtime, I came to appreciate life in Haiti with my auntie and the small things I once took for granted, like the privacy of her home, having very few visitors who lingered, going to school with my sister, praying and attending Sunday mass. Most of all, I missed having someone else to talk to.

It became my responsibility to clean, cook, and maintain the home. Although my stepsister—the faceless girl helped it seemed that I carried most of the responsibilities because I was home the more. I was living the life that Madame Marcel had predicted for me, but this wasn't Madame Marcel's doing—it was my mother's doing.

Living with Mother came with many expectations and the conditions were becoming unbearable. I resented having so much chaos surrounding us, which included the many fights between Mother and

Stepfather. Most of the time, she was gone from home, she was more like a visitor. Life was difficult and hard for all of us it seemed, but particularly the women.

It was hard for them to find work, unlike the men who were able to drive taxis. My mother and many of her women friends resorted to playing cards, trying to win money to help support their families. Whenever there was a card game, Mother was sure to find it, or they would find her. This wasn't what I thought life would be like in the Caribbean for my mother.

I was puzzled by the constant flow of people coming in and out of our home, even though I understood Mother and Stepfather's need to make money, and her need to find something to do. I often wished those people wouldn't come around. It was hard for me to understand why the women couldn't find something else other than play cards, day in, and day out.

I began to understand the difference between the realities and fantasies of life in the Caribbean. The stories my sister and I heard about while living in Haiti—about people in the Caribbean living richly—were not true, at least not for my mother, her family or their friends. What was true was that life in the Caribbean was hard. I learned that being a stranger in a foreign country, being an outsider came with many disadvantages and disappointments. Surviving sometimes meant forgetting their pride and dignity for the chance that someday their situation would turn around, if not for themselves, for their children.

My days in the Caribbean were as uncomfortable as one would have expected. Occasionally on the weekends, my stepfather would take us to the beach for some fun and to search for sea grapes. And I would enjoy each of those outings, seeing the beautiful beaches and the tourists.

During the week while my stepsister was in school, I was at home, responsible for the chores, which sometimes included cooking. I remember the day I tried cooking a special dinner, our famous black rice, I wanted to please stepfather. When he returned home that day from his driving job; dinner was ready and the table set for him. It was a ritual to get it right. Plastic containers were not allowed at the table and everything had to be set neatly with proper utensils, napkins, and freshly squeezed lemonade or grapefruit juices.

The mistake I made was in cooking the black rice, forgetting to remove the mushroom pulps, which gave the rice its color, and use only the liquid. When I served it to him, he was visibly upset because I did not cook the rice correctly. I remember escaping a beating that day for not doing it right, I was grateful.

The more I learned about my new family, the more I missed Haiti. However, I also knew that being in the Caribbean was the best place for me at that time. I did everything required of me so that I wouldn't be sent back to Haiti.

Although at times the situations were harsh, I prayed that things would get better, and tried patiently waiting for when I would be at school. I felt strangely different when I was alone, while my stepsister attended school.

The circumstances by which I had arrived in the Caribbean made it quite difficult for me to attend school right away. My options were limited while Mother tried everything to get my documents, until she could pay someone to get my birth records and bring them back from Haiti. In the meantime, I stayed home, wanting to be like all the other children in school, and to be like my stepsister.

IX
AMONG STRANGERS

One aspect that became very apparent early on was how very little time Mother had to devote to us. She was expecting another child and seemed preoccupied with other events in her life. She was barely there emotionally or physically, I felt as though I were living among strangers. Although, in some respects, we were all strangers to each other, when she was physically present, it was as though she were not there at all, preoccupied with responsibilities.

Among their friends, there was one of them in particular who was consistently nice to me. His name was Gabriel. He visited our home quite often and always brought us sweets. He went out of his way to be extra nice to me, and showed me a bit more attention than he did to my stepsister. He stood up for me when others teased or taunted me about my darker skin. He made them stop and then followed with a compliment. He told me how pretty I was and that I shouldn't listen to those people who made fun of me. I was very happy when he was around because he made me feel special.

Whenever "Uncle Gabe" came around, I would be the first one to run and greet him. He would pick me up and embraced me just as I imagined a father would embrace his child. He showed me more kindness than my stepfather ever had. He wasn't like all the others who paraded through our home: He didn't play cards as often as they did, and he spent more time observing than playing with Stepsister and me. Other times, he sat with her and me to watch television in the living room. That is, when we weren't running around fetching drinks and food. Sometimes, he sat Stepsister and me on his lap to tell us stories.

It was during one of those story times that he said I was like the daughter he never had, and even though I knew he wasn't my father, those words made me feel special. He made up a name just for me—*Lapin*. At the time, I didn't know what it meant (rabbit), but just the same, I liked it very much. That name was just for me. He didn't have a special name for Stepsister. For the first time, I felt I had something that she couldn't take from me. Whenever he called me *Lapin*, I felt extra special. I enjoyed the attention he gave me and I liked that whenever he was around, he made me feel as if I were the most important person in our home. Since he was Mother and Stepfather's very good friend, I thought that if they saw how special he thought I was and how he treated me, maybe they would treat me as special, too.

Slowly over time, as the newness of being in the Caribbean wore faded. I began noticing some changes in Uncle Gabe's behavior toward me. He did little things that made me feel strange. When I sat on his lap, he looked down my dress and whispered comments in my ear about how my as-yet-undeveloped breasts looked. Those comments made me uncomfortable but didn't seem out of the ordinary. Others in the household routinely made the same type of remarks aloud in passing. I noticed other strange behaviors, such as how he attempted to run his hands across my chest and then he rubbed me there. He tried to play tickling games and kiss me on the lips, but I turned away. Even though I felt uncomfortable with his actions, I pushed my feelings aside. In my mind, I wanted to believe he would never do anything to hurt me because he told me I was like the daughter he never had.

His behavior was becoming more forceful. He would place his hand on my knee, then in my lap, and then slowly he would try to move his hand under my dress. I was constantly pushing him away to make him stop. Deep inside, I knew that what he was doing was wrong, yet I convinced myself that I was making a mountain out of a molehill. How, I reasoned, could he do something that was wrong when so many other people were around?

Other times, he put his hand on my private parts and even though other adults were around playing cards, only a few feet away, they seemed unable to see what he was doing—at least that was my justification why they never said anything. When I replay his boldness and the images in my mind, I was puzzled by his actions and their inaction. Wondering why they would ignore him when what he was doing seemed wrong? This was very difficult for me to handle , even years later, but I rationalized that perhaps Mother, Stepfather, and the other adults nearby never said anything because they didn't know that he was doing those things. Thinking back, I remember that when they played cards, their backs or sides were turned away from Uncle and me because of the way the dining table was positioned in the corner of the room and the way the sofa was arranged to divide two rooms.

Regularly, I tried to get away from him during those uncomfortable moments. I shifted and moved his hand away from my body and changed seats, but he followed me as if we were playing a game. Although he would eventually stop, I didn't question his behavior or ask Stepsister if he did the same things to her. The more he continued to come around, the more uncomfortable I became. All the things he had said before about my being like a daughter no longer made me feel special. I tried to avoid him. I didn't like anything about him anymore. He was supposed to protect me, and I felt he had let me down. I hated it when he called me *Lapin*. I think he realized that I didn't look up to him as I once did. I was afraid of him and of the strange ways he looked at me.

Days before my tenth birthday, Mother gave birth to a baby boy—my baby brother. Having a baby brother was a gift from God. The day he was born was one of the happiest of my life. I knew that I had a brother who was part of me, who was part of the *real* family I had longed for, given that I had never felt part of my mother's new family. My stepfather didn't accept me, and most of the time, Mother was like a stranger. There was no connection.

X

A BABY TO LOVE

Having a baby brother was like a dream come true, he meant the world to me. I wanted, and needed to feel important by helping Mother with his care, I wanted him to be my own to care for, but Mother had included Stepsister in caring for the baby.

The day my baby brother came home from the hospital, I felt connected to him, maybe because of my desire to feel needed and wanted, and my desire to give someone all the love I had in me to give and he was just perfect. I believed he would love me back. I had not felt that family connection with anyone else, except my sister, when we lived together in Haiti. The connection with my sister eventually fell apart, because we had not seen each other, only in passing. I felt lost and lonely without her, but now I had my baby brother to take away that loneliness and sadness.

I wanted to do everything for him that Mother had asked of me, so that I would keep him safe. I wanted Mother to be proud of me for taking good care of him; I never wanted to disappoint her. I wanted the baby to be mine. After all, he and I were of the same mother, which, in my mind, meant that I had more rights to him than she did.

He was the most handsome baby boy, he looked pink and pale with a head full of soft, curly black hair. He looked like an angel. He was my angel. I became a mother to him, and looked after him the way I wished Mother had looked after me. I felt responsible for him just as my sister had been for me in Haiti, and on the many occasion when he and I were left alone while Mother and Stepfather were out trying to find ways to provide for us, Stepsister and I were put in charge of the house and caring for the baby.

Even when Mother was home, he was still our responsibility—more mine than Stepsister's, because I was home with him most of the time while she was in school. Most nights, when the baby awakened or when mother was just arriving home from a very long, long day, she would wake one of us or both of us to feed him, change his *nappy*, to get him back to sleep before we could return to our beds.

Most nights, Mother would be tired, especially on those long days before from being gone. When she was at home, if neither Stepsister or I responded to my brother's cry, she would get very mad and stormed into our room, so that we would attend to the baby, other times she would grab me by the hair, and forced me out of bed to get the baby's bottle and change him.

Most of the time, Stepsister would escape the brunt of her anger. There were certain things Stepfather wouldn't allow, so I suffered the brunt of Mother's rage and anger. Most nights, though, I would jump out of bed at the sound of a pin drop to rush to my brother's crib, making sure he was fed and changed so I wouldn't get smacked. Some days I would be so tired that I couldn't even force myself to get into the bathroom for my bath. I knew that when Mother came home, if she saw that we hadn't bathed—no matter what the time was—she would take her slipper and beat us to the bath. Whether it was Stepsister or me on the receiving end, there were plenty to go around.

Stepsister and I were very much on the same path when it came to Mother, we dared not disturbed her sleep on those rare nights. It was as if we were programmed to respond immediately to the sounds of our brother. We made sure that he never cried long enough, we were afraid that Mother might upset. Stepsister and I took turns feeding him at night. Sometimes we would bend over his crib until we fell asleep with him.

My dream of what life with Mother would be like after our reunion didn't match my reality. In many ways, it seemed much worse than I had imagined. I often wished I were back in Haiti with my sister Marsha, but I knew I had to be strong, because things would eventually get better.

Every night before I went to sleep, I prayed that my brother would never have to endure my suffering. I prayed that he would never feel abandoned and unwanted as I did. Most of all, I prayed that he would never have to question our mother's love for him as I had done so many times. I planned on giving him all the love I had in me to give and through him; I hoped to experience the love we both needed. I wanted to ensure he had happiness in his young life.

XI

HOPELESS

It seemed that there were always something going on in our home, there was a constant flow of people day in and day out, I remember most the smoking and loud talking all the time. Our home seemed to be the place where they would all come to play cards. I hated that everyone always came unannounced. I became very unhappy very quickly, but that unhappiness was accepted as a part of life.

Mother seemed always to be the pressured of having to provide a good home, under the circumstances. Now that she had three children to feed, the tension between her and Stepfather was increasingly uncomfortable, it was the usually insulted and arguments about money. Their constant bickering wasn't enough to keep them apart, though because wherever Stepfather went, Mother was sure to follow, and vice versa. They enjoyed the excitement of the card games.

Although Mother made many attempts to find other means of work, she was never able so, so the games became her way of earning the income she needed. She was always creative in trying different things and one of those ways was in preparing food to sell to her friends. She would wake up early to prepare the food; day after day, she repeated the same routine. She also tried setting up a small shop in our home to sell cigarettes, fresh-squeezed juice and blended drinks, perfumes, soaps, and just about anything that would bring in extra money so that she would no longer have to play cards. For a while, she had done well, but not for long.

The same people kept coming around our home, even though she tried to stop playing cards, she and Stepfather allow them to play, because she would be able to sell food to them while they were there. They seemed to come around more than ever before. They'd stay for a casual game that would turn into an all-day, all-night event. They left only when they ran out of money or credit, when they could no longer stay awake, or when Mother asked them to leave.

Some of them would give her a very small portion of their winnings for allowing them to play in our home. Nevertheless, as time went on, Mother just could not stand by watching everyone else having all the fun. She became frustrated seeing the time and money she had put into trying a restaurant business go to waste, she was losing money from selling the food. People were buying everything on credit with promised to pay when they had money or winnings, but very few of them did.

Although she tried staying away from the card table, having the same people in our home made it impossible for her to stop completely. Watching those people play, while she slaved over a hot stove all day cooking food that people were not paying for became more of a hassle.

Eventually, Mother stopped cooking and went back to playing cards. Some nights, she and Stepfather come home only to check on us and to make sure we had food to eat. They would be gone again, and on those days when she or Stepfather could not check on us, they would send their friends—usually Uncle Gabe—to do so and to bring food and milk for the baby. They would ask Uncle Gabe; because he was the one they seem to trust the most. I hated the sight of him; I hated when he came to our home, knowing that I couldn't voice my concerns to anyone or keep him from being there.

The compliments he had been giving me no longer held the same meaning for me. He continued with his acts against me, making me feel strange and uneasy. On his many visits to our home, I would try my best to avoid him. However, I would be called out of my room for one reason or another—to get a glass of water or food while they played cards. He would stand there with them, trying to be normal, as if he were a good person. He would call me that name I came to dislike so very much.

His routines were always the same, whenever Stepsister and I were watching television, he would sit between us. He would stroke our backs or stroke our hair with his hand, as one would do with a puppy. I would move his hands away or try ducking, to keep him from touching me, but that never seemed to work.

He would look at me strangely and at time accused me of being *dezòd*. He would act as if I had done something wrong. I was afraid of Mother's reaction if she thought I that I was being rude to him, so I would just sit there and pretend that nothing was wrong. My thoughts would often drift elsewhere, distracting myself by focusing on the television. I would freeze when he touched me, while the other adults were seemingly unaware of what he was doing.

He would position himself on the sofa, so that no one would see his hands, unless they were standing directly behind the sofa. He would place his hand under my dress many times. I would try getting away from him, but was usually unsuccessful. When I was able to get away, I would rush to my room, once there; I would sit on my bed and cry. Sometimes during those routine visits, if I were in my room, he would go looking for me; he would take my hands and place them inside his pants, and forced me to rub his body parts. He would caution me not to tell anyone. I hated all of those things he made me do. I hated the odor on my hands afterward. I tried to avoid him every chance I got, but the situation at home encouraged him to be there.

I am not sure if anyone saw past his pretences, everyone thought he was a nice man; he was there very good friend and he always pretended to be nice to me, so they didn't understand my sudden dislike for him. They also didn't understand why I moved away whenever he came near me. Sometimes I would be reprimanded for not embracing him or greeting anyone who came to our home. As a result, I stopped running from him. I didn't want to get in more trouble, or get punished for being disrespectful to him or anyone else.

I remember all the times he forced me to sit on his lap. He grabbed me under my arms and placed his hands on my "undeveloped breasts," as he often referred to them, and felt me up. It was a constant struggle for me to keep him away. I kept hoping that someone would see him, see what he was doing, yet I was afraid of getting punished if I said anything. He pretended to be playing with Stepsister and me, and sometimes he would threaten to spank us both if we misbehaved.

With so many people coming in and out of our home at all hours, it was impossible to feel safe. Every corner of our home was packed with people. Stepsister and I tried to stay out of their way by retreating to our room, but we couldn't avoid them.

I became very reclusive and afraid of him, withdrawn from my family. I hated my home. I hated my life, and I hated feeling sad all the time. His acts escalated and became more frequent, and the shame followed me for years. I believed that I couldn't stop his actions.

XII

INNOCENCE LOST

Being responsible for my baby brother was my only joy living at home. He was my companion, the one I would talk to, even though he couldn't talk back, my escape from the dismal reality to which I had been shoved into. My brother made all of my worries disappear when we were together. He made things seem normal even when they weren't.

It was during one of those many routine visits Uncle Gabe paid me while everyone was away that have haunted me. On that day, he had come to check on my brother and me. Mother had left by midafternoon on her quest, Stepfather was out driving his taxi, Stepsister had gone to school, and I stayed home with my brother, while still waiting for the documents from Haiti that would allow me to enter school in the Caribbean. Uncle Gabe had arrived earlier to take Mother to her destination; but by afternoon, he had returned, because he said Mother had asked him to see how we were doing. Such midday visits weren't unusual.

I remember him knocking on the back door to the kitchen and called out that name—*Lapin*—asking that I opened the door. I wished it had been someone else. I didn't want to open the door, but I knew that I had to. I walked to the door and unlocked it, hoping he would leave right away after handing me the container of food that Mother had sent him to deliver, and after seeing that my brother and I were okay. He pushed his way past me and cautiously entered the kitchen. He pulled the door closed behind him, sauntering into the dining area and sat at the table. I kept my distance and stood between the hallway and the kitchen.

He questioned me about my brother and then headed toward the room where my brother was napping. He walked past me, looking around, while checking the other rooms and then the bathroom. Shortly afterward, he went into the living room and then to the dining room. I remember feeling strangely trapped, although I was still standing, frozen, between the kitchen and the hallway. He sat at the dining table, stared at me, and for awhile, said nothing. In the silence, I focused my attention on the television, which I had been watching, but now he was watching me.

I prayed he would leave.

I said nothing.

Afraid to speak, I said nothing.

I was afraid of him being in the house.

I said nothing.

I wondered quietly to myself about his piercing looks in my direction.

In my mind, I screamed with fear. Yet, I said nothing.

Who would hear me?

We were in the house alone with my baby brother and the television.

I prayed Mother or Stepfather would come home so he would leave. Yet, I still said nothing. I didn't want to speak to him. I didn't want him to look at me, yet he was looking.

I held still. I felt afraid to breathe because I feared moving. I feared he would notice I was there. I wanted to be invisible to him, and to his gaze.

I stood against the wall in complete stillness, in silence, and allowed the television to blare away. Then he broke the silence and stillness I had tried so valiantly to maintain.

He spoke.

I said nothing.

I was afraid he might notice me standing against the wall.

I said nothing.

Yet he noticed me anyway.

Still, I said nothing.

My mind and heart raced until I heard my brother's cry and reacted in surprise.

Yet, I said nothing.

Uncle Gabe called me that name again, as I stood against the wall and contemplated my options—do I go to my brother or continue to stand in the hallway, waiting for *him* to leave?

He called me that name again—the only name he had ever called me since he had made it up. That name I associated only with him—*Lapin*.

I quickly glanced in his direction with a sudden feeling of shock, yet I said nothing.

I slowly slid against the wall, trying to make my way to the bedroom where my brother's cries had grown louder. I watched to make sure he wasn't following me, but he was.

I walked quickly to the room, but his steps were faster.

I rushed to push the door shut, but he placed his hand in the way.

I rushed to my brother's crib, as if he would be the shield between *him* and me—the shield that would keep him from touching me again.

I was still too afraid that he might do something if I spoke.

I said nothing while the tears trickled down my face.

I felt confined as he stood on the other side of the room, blocking the doorway.

I was afraid he might move toward me, and I hoped that the baby's crying would make him leave.

I said nothing.

He remained in front of the door, guarding it. Then he sat at the foot of the bed.

I said nothing.

He sat there on the bed watching me as I fed my brother his bottle.

I said nothing.

I hoped he would leave, and I wished that someone would come home.

I said nothing.

He spoke and all I heard were the muttering sounds emanating from his mouth.

My mind was overwhelmed with thoughts, panic and anxiety; while my heart began to beat violently.

I said nothing.

He spoke, but I couldn't make out what he was saying. I was lost in my fears, unable to breathe. I was hyperventilating, and my heart pounded with anxiety.

I said nothing.

I said nothing.

I focused my attention on feeding my brother as he lay in his crib. Uncle Gabe walked over to where I stood near the crib. He stood beside me and observed me, as if to make sure the baby was actually in the crib. All along, I had hoped that he wouldn't come near me, because I didn't want him to see that the bottle was actually empty and that the baby was only sucking on air bubbles, but he did. He grabbed my arms and tried to pull me away from the crib, but I reached and grabbed the crib's railing and held on tightly.

It was a tug of war between us—a tug of war for my safety, but I was never safe with him in our home. No one else was there to make him stop, and I wouldn't let go of the crib without a fight. He pulled and I held onto the crib with all I had in me. He grabbed me harder and pulled again. I held onto the rails and hoped they were strong enough to keep me from harm. Then he grabbed me by my waist. I remember feeling the crib rolling with me as I refused to let go. I prayed that Mother would walk through the door and see what he was doing, and maybe then, she wouldn't think he was such a nice person.

I cried, screamed, and kicked, hoping he would let go of me—hoping he would give up. During the struggle, he attempted with great force to unlock my fingers and to pull me away from the crib. Although my will was strong, my strength was no match for his. My kicking and screaming didn't matter to him, but I didn't let up. I kicked and screamed some more and tried to free myself from his grip. I thought that the baby's cry combined with mine would make him stop, but he ignored us both and continued his violation of my innocence.

He pushed me down on the bed that my stepsister and I had shared since moving to the new duplex. When I tried to free myself from beneath him, he placed his arm across my body and shoulders, and held me down. He placed a hand over my mouth to quiet my cries, and then he pushed my dress above my waist.

I remember collapsing under the pressure of his body on top of mine. I felt exhausted from crying and from trying to fight him. I remember lying there, but being absent from my body, trying to pretend that what he was doing wasn't happening to me, and that he wasn't doing those things to me. I sobbed, and pleaded for him to stop hurting me.

While he violated me, he continued to speak, but his words were muffled with the sound of my cries that were deaf to his idle chatter.

He grabbed at my undeveloped breasts. He grabbed at me. He palmed me like one might sift through loose feed for the pigs.

I remember wishing I were dead. The way he had me pinned under him, I couldn't move, and I couldn't make him stop.

Through it all, my brother lay in his crib crying, yet *he* didn't care. He had no regard for either of us.

He continued his course of derailment, and then amidst it all, he tried to justify his actions.

"I won't hurt you. I won't make you bleed," he said.

Again, his words were muffled by the sound of my brother's and my cries. A hot stream of tears ran down my cheeks.

"I won't hurt you. I won't make you bleed," he continued saying. "No one will know."

He unzipped his pants as he held me down with his body.

He tried to put his tongue in my mouth, but I clenched my teeth and turned my face.

While trying to kick and fight, he pulled down my panties and violated my private with his hand. I tried pushing his hand away, but I couldn't, the more I fought him, the more he was hurt me. Then he did the unthinkable, he removed his hand, pinned my ten-year-old body beneath him, shoving his private into me. I screamed in agony.

He kept saying, "I won't hurt you. I won't make you bleed," he said.

Sobbing uncontrollably, I pleaded for him to stop.

He spoke again, saying, "Little girls are sweet."

I felt sick and prayed, as I gasped for air, that God would take my life.

"Don't worry," he said repeatedly. "I won't make you bleed."

The room felt as if it were spinning. My breathing faltered because of the weight of him on my battered body.

"*Lapin*," he said.

Suddenly something made him stop. He got up and went to the toilet. I lay there crying, not knowing what else to do, and then he returned to the room.

He spoke again, and this time he ordered me to wash. He reminded me that I had better not tell anyone about what he had done.

He told me why it was important that I not tell anyone, particularly my mother. He said that Mother would be disappointed if she found out that I had let him do those things to me. He told me Mother would send me back to Haiti, and that no one would believe me.

He told me it was my fault that he did those things and he told me that I had forced him to do them.

He said that I was sweet. He said that little girls were sweet.

He said that it was our secret.

He said if I told anyone, he would have his friends deport me back to Haiti because of the way I came to the Caribbean--in the banana-boat.

He violated me. I was ten years old.

Shaken by the ordeal, I slowly walked to the toilet and washed myself as he had ordered. I wanted to get rid of his smell, the unpleasant odor on my clothes and skin. I felt dirty and I felt that I had committed a sin against God.

I wanted my sister more than ever. I needed her protection. I wanted her to hold me and tell me that everything would be okay again.

I wanted her to tell me that it wasn't my fault, but most of all, I cried for my mother.

I cried and said nothing.

Everything he said had sounded convincing. Perhaps I did lead him to do all those things he said. Perhaps it was my fault. I couldn't tell or ask anyone to help, not even my mother. He said never to speak of his crimes. He said that he would make sure that no one knew.

His words replayed themselves in my mind.

The way he repeated them, "You are sweet."

"Little girls like you are sweet."

"Yeah," he said.

"I didn't make you bleed."

I sobbed and thought about the embarrassment, the shame, and Mother's reaction if she found out. I knew what he did to me was never supposed to happen. Auntie always talked about how young ladies should never do such things until marriage, and Mother would say the same. I was certain that I would be blamed and punished for his acts against me. My family would chastise and ostracize me. They would call me names. They wouldn't see me as a child who had been violated, but as a girl who was fast and loose, infected and impure.

He left the same way he came—through the back door to the kitchen—like a thief in the daylight, he left me carrying his guilt and shame.

The disappointment...they trusted him. I had trusted him.

I was only ten years old.

XIII

INFERNO

Mother and Stepfather had engaged in numerous exchanges of unpleasant words—name-calling and accusations that the other had been involved in having affairs. On this day, though, Mother had had enough. On the advice of friends, and feeling quite hurt, she decided to leave Stepfather once and for all. Their arrangement was no longer working for them. They constantly bickered about money, the bills, his drunken escapades, and the public humiliation she experienced when he, when intoxicated, called her names.

Mother could no longer put up with the insults and his constant disrespect. His actions toward her and his humiliation of her in front of their friends made Mother the most angry, but she was never one to back down from a good fight. Mother had learned that Stepfather had a woman friend who was rumored to be his "special" woman friend. It all made perfect sense to Mother now. The evidence she needed to confirm her suspicion was Stepfather's strange behavior during the previous months. Now she knew why he never seemed to have any money. Her discovery of his affair was accompanied by mutual verbal combat and insults.

After their quarrels, Stepfather would stay away and not return home. One night, after such a quarrel, instead of coming home, the neighbors informed Mother that Stepfather had spent the night at the woman's home—the same woman friend they had fought about the evening before, and the same woman he had repeatedly denied having relations with.

That morning, when Mother awoke, she was once again alerted that Stepfather had stayed the night with his woman friend. The friend lived only doors away from our home. Father apparently had gone there undetected because he had parked his taxi in a male friend's backyard so it would look as if he had spent the entire night at his male friend's home.

I remember Mother's rage that morning, and her expressions of betrayal. Mother rushed to the woman's home, hoping that what she had learned was untrue. To her surprise, though, he was there, just as the others had alleged. I remember watching the events unfold from our front yard. Stepsister and I had followed Mother out the door that morning. We watched as she marched over to the woman's house. Mother didn't have time to knock on the door and wait for an answer. Instead, she woke the household up by throwing a brick through the front window. Mother demanded that Stepfather come out of the woman's home. She demanded that the woman leave Stepfather alone.

As soon as the brick smashed the window, Stepfather came stumbling out in dismay, surprised. He wanted to know who would be so bold as to throw a brick through the window. He wondered if Mother had lost her mind, and more to the point, how Mother had found out where he had been all night. He was surprised beyond words to find her standing on the front steps, hands on her hips—her usual position when she was preparing for battle—shouting at both the woman and him about their betrayal.

He called out her name, as if pleading with her. His shirt, which he apparently had grabbed and put on in a hurry, was unbuttoned. His very round belly protruded from the opening. The woman remained inside, looking out through the broken front window at the spectacle unfolding on her front steps. A crowd began to form. The situation was both embarrassing and amusing. To add salt to Mother's wounds, Stepfather insulted her once again in front of the woman's home, with everyone watching. He exploded, and told Mother that he didn't want her anymore, and that it was over between them. He made it clear to Mother that he was moving on. There he was in public, berating the mother of his child, the woman who had cared for his daughter, and the woman he found no longer useful or sufficient for his needs.

It was apparent to everyone watching that his words had cut deeply into Mother like a dull blade slicing painfully through her heart. Tears rolled down her cheeks as she called his name, painfully repeating what she had heard from his lips. The pain of watching Mother in such distress and being humiliated so publicly was devastating. Even as a child, although I didn't fully understand the implications of their words and actions, my heart ached for Mother. I, too, felt her pain and embarrassment.

His comments were heard by all, and his actions didn't go unnoticed. Most of their friends suggested they both return home to resolve their issues for the sake of their children. However, many of the women present added more fuel to Mother's already raging fire. To make matters worse, the alleged girlfriend decided to come to Stepfather's defense. The screaming and shouting continued. Bystanders ducked as shoes and sandals whizzed past them. Everyone tried to keep Mother from attacking the woman. If she had, it wouldn't have been a pretty sight. The alleged girlfriend had her own agenda. Unexpectedly, she hiked up her nightgown, pulled down her panties, and mooned Mother. When that happened, it was as if the sky had opened up with a thundering roar. The confrontation exploded.

The spectators couldn't believe their eyes as Mother expressed her anger. She was furious with Stepfather for causing this situation and allowing the woman—who had once been a mutual friend—to disrespect Mother in such a manner. She demanded that Stepfather move out of their home immediately. Both spoke bitter words that they could never take back. Both had broken promises that could never be mended, and our lives would never be the same.

That afternoon, Stepfather returned and parked his taxi in the front yard, hoping that the storm had calmed. Still in a rage, Mother slashed the tires with a large knife as he had cut through her heart. His taxi, his only means for work, his only source of transportation, stood disabled in our front yard. Mother wanted to make sure that Stepfather felt her pain and her wrath, and if he ever had any doubts about the lengths she would go to be heard and understood, he would know now. She continued her storm, smashing through every window on the taxi, knowing that even if he managed to replace the tires, he still wouldn't be able to use the automobile for work. Mother's devastation yielded results that were even more shocking. It wasn't enough that she had destroyed Stepfather's automobile. She wanted to cause him great pain and anguish.

To this day, I can recall the details so very clearly. I have never forgotten the fury in Mother's eyes, and the rage that shook her voice and body. She became like a wild tornado, gathering strength in her destruction as she threw all of his belongings—every stitch of clothing he owned, including his shoes, underwear, socks, and cologne—into a big metal barrel next to his battered car. She emptied out all the contents of his drawers, and dumped everything into the barrel, filling it to the top. Then came her moment of true insanity, she lit a cigarette to calm her nerves, poured gasoline over the items in the barrel, and used her cigarette to set the items ablaze.

The news of her actions traveled faster than an electrical charge, and Stepfather came running home, hoping to stop her behavior that had already taken a drastic course. His attempts to salvage his belongings failed miserably. He had run up against my Mother's will and determination, which was stronger than his own. He tried confronting Mother and was on the receiving end of her unwavering anger. The fire that burned inside her was like the one in the barrel—hot and heavy. Just like the spectacle earlier that day, people lined up around our yard, watching as the events unfolded.

Stepfather and Mother exchanged words again, and they became objects of mockery and ridicule as the neighbors looked on. He attempted to enter our home to confront Mother, but her fire had not diminished. She didn't want to hear his complaints nor his excuses. In another violent rage—to be rid of him once and for all—she ripped the front of what was his only shirt left; the one he had been wearing. His only possessions now were half of a shirt and the pants and shoes he was wearing. Mother had burned everything else. That afternoon, Mother, our neighbors, Stepsister and me witnessed Stepfather's tears. He wept for the things he held dear, watching helplessly as nearly everything he owned burned to the ground.

As the charred remains of his belongings turned to ash in the front yard, some of the ashes escaped the barrel, prompting neighbors to call the authorities and fire brigade. They dowsed the remaining ashes with water, but by then, the fi re had dissipated. Only the smoke from the now wet ashes filled the air. The authorities questioned the neighbors and then spoke to Mother and Stepfather. They handed Mother some papers and told her to report downtown. Rumors were that Uncle Gabe's persuaded the authorities from carting Mother away. The evening ended. Mother had escaped possible deportation for vandalizing Stepfather's taxi and setting the fire.

XVI

THE ESCAPE

Shortly after that volatile incident between Mother and Stepfather, she decided to leave the Caribbean permanently. Stepfather was no longer living in our home, Mother decided to set her plan into motion. She thought that this was her best chance to leave, with my baby brother and me, because he wouldn't be returning. Her plan included our secret flight to Florida to start over. Few people knew of mother's plan, including Uncle Gabe and me.

Her decision to leave was difficult, particularly because she had to leave Stepsister behind. She was afraid that Stepfather might accuse her of kidnapping his daughter. When I learned that Stepsister wouldn't be traveling with us, a part of me felt victorious. I would no longer walk in her shadows. I was happy to be the one leaving with Mother this time around. I was happy to have been the chosen one on this journey. A small part of me, though, missed Stepsister already.

Mother made the arrangements for our departure and assigned a family friend to look after Stepsister on the day we would leave. Mother didn't want Stepfather to be alerted to her plan until our airplane was safely off the ground. She ensured that her plan would allow us enough time to get to the plane and prevent Stepfather from stopping us or notifying the authorities, given that we were traveling without proper documents again.

The night before our departure, Mother locked all the doors and windows and called me into her bedroom. There, she retrieved a very large square can from beneath the bed covers in the closet. The can was tall, large, and heavy. Using a sharp knife, she cut through the welded lid and poured the content on the ground.

I was mesmerized by the sight of money pouring out of the can. Mother and I knelt on the floor and watched the coins pour out. There was money everywhere; more money than I had ever seen before. It was as if it were pouring rain. I thought that we were rich. I saw silver coins, paper money of many colors, large bills, and small bills. As the money poured on the floor, Mother explained that it was a combination of her winnings from the card games, and from playing the numbers—the Haitian equivalent of the lottery. She had collected all the money over the years from paying into the *esso*—the Haitians' equivalent of a savings account; which back then, they didn't believe in putting their money into a bank accounts, for fear that they wouldn't be able to get it in an emergency. The *esso* gave members an opportunity to get an instant loan by taking bi-weekly turns in getting what was collected between them. When it was Mother's turn to collect, she had simply saved the money.

Together we counted the money and separated the coins from the paper money. Mother counted the paper money while I counted the coins. We counted pile after pile. The money covered a small corner of Mother's bedroom. For the first time ever, counting the money with

Mother gave me something to hold onto—something to share with the woman who had been a stranger to me. It was the first time I felt close to Mother since I had come to live with her and know her. That was the only time that we had been entirely alone together, with my brother joining us; it all seemed so perfect. That night, Mother and I counted several thousands of dollars, which she used to buy our one-way tickets to freedom—our tickets to Florida.

That night, we couldn't sleep. Both of us were worried about the journey ahead and the outcome. I was afraid, and Mother was nervously packing the small bags we would take with us. Mother planned to leave everything she owned behind for those friends and family who knew of our departure. She packed little clothing for herself and a small bag, with bottles and food, for my baby brother. Others had instructed Mother to avoid overloading the small airplane with unnecessary baggage. After sorting and packing, we tried to rest, but the anticipation of the trip was overwhelming. Before the sun rose, we were ready for our journey.

Outside, Uncle Gabe waited in his automobile to take us to the secret location where we were to board the small airplane. Seeing him again, for what would be the last time, reminded me of his loathsome acts against me. The rape came rushing back to me like a speeding train. I stood frozen in place as I replayed that train wreck in my mind. It would be the last time I would ever have to worry about him hurting me again.

Mother's voice broke my reverie as she encouraged me to hurry for our journey. Mother, the baby, and I climbed into his automobile and drove to the meeting location. During the entire trip, he continued to glance at me in the rearview mirror, trying to make eye contact. On our arrival, we quickly prepared to board, but not before Uncle Gabe approached and embraced me one last time. Although I tried backing away, I didn't want to appear impolite in front of my mother. He leaned over and whispered into my ear. He told me that I must never tell anyone about what he said was our secret. I pulled away as soon as the pilot whistled for us to board.

That day, I believed in my heart that I would no longer have to fear him again.

With my mother's savings, we headed for Florida. Again, like thieves in the night, we left our past and shattered existence behind.

The sun had risen and the airplane slowly descended to a wooded field, in an open space. After landing, the pilot quickly turned off the motor and gave us specific instructions to ensure our safety and to make certain the authorities wouldn't detect us. Although we had landed, we remained seated inside until we had received the signal that it was safe to unload. On signal, we quickly exited the airplane and rushed to a waiting automobile, which took us to another meeting place. There, family members were supposed to meet us.

Mother carried the baby while grasping my arm as we hurried across the field to the automobile. When we arrived at the other meeting place—someone's home—several other people were there waiting for their families coming from other locations. On entering the house, Mother recognized one of the men. They greeted each other and he quickly escorted us to his automobile and drove away. The man was one of mother's brothers, my Uncle Harry. That day we were free immigrants once again, but this time in America.

Uncle Harry drove us to his home. There, we met his wife, Auntie Angel, and their children. They lived in a white brick home. Auntie Angel welcomed us with a hot meal, and throughout the day, other family members came to visit us. News circulated that Mother had landed with her children, as in Haiti, and again, in the Caribbean. I met people whose faces I had not seen and others from previous encounters in the Caribbean. Every day, someone new visited, and the visits lasted for weeks. Like before, the excitement about being in a new country eventually wore off.

A few things were different from life in the Caribbean. In Florida, Mother would be able to work during the day. She had been out looking for work, and sometimes at night, Uncle Harry would take her to card games. Mother's efforts in finding work eventually paid off sooner than she had expected. She found part-time work at a diner washing dishes in the evenings. Shortly afterward, she found another job working for a laundry service company. Since arriving, Mother was like a different person. She was now working two jobs to save money for a house, whereas before, she felt she had to play cards and sell food to make a living. I was able to attend the school near my uncle's home. I was elated! In the evening, when mother left for her night job, Auntie Angel would come home from her job in time to watch my brother and me. Life was different; Mother rarely left us alone. In the Caribbean, her life had been consumed by her constant need to play cards to support us. This time, though, she had no such need to leave us alone.

XV

THE REUNION

I enjoyed having Mother's time to myself, although she made scheduled weekend calls to Stepsister to be sure that she was being properly cared for. Most of the time, Mother spoke with Stepfather, the topic of conversation was Mother's abrupt departure.

Frequently, the calls would end in a disagreement. Those types of calls became routine. The more Mother called, the more distraught she became. At times, Stepfather would plead with her to help him to get to Florida so he could see his son. He would request money from her so that he would pay people he owed—people who had been threatening to hurt him if he didn't pay them. He said that he also needed money to repair his badly damaged taxi. He told Mother how he had been unable to work. He told her how badly things were going for him. He told Mother how much he missed her and how much he wanted to see his children, including me, when before I had always been an afterthought.

It was during those many calls, that he asked his cousin Sam to speak to Mother on his behalf, to help encourage her to give him another chance. Sam started coming over to Uncle's home on a regular basis. He and Uncle were also friends back in the Caribbean. Sam became the buffer between Mother and Stepfather.

I prayed that she wouldn't change her mind and give him another chance. I liked that Mother had been home more often and was working. For the first time, I was enjoying life—just the three of us plus the closeness Mother and I shared.

Stepfather called constantly, begging and pleading for Mother's forgiveness, for another chance. Eventually, Mother told him the news; the she was nearly five months' pregnant. It was because of her pregnancy that Uncle Harry persuaded her to help Stepfather travel to Florida, to give him another chance. Uncle Harry and his cousin Sam influenced her decision.

Uncle Harry believed that a married woman should be with her husband, and because Mother was expecting another child, he didn't feel that she should have the child alone. He told Mother that she needed to be with her husband for the sake of her children. Together, Mother and Uncle Harry raised the money Stepfather needed to pay his way to Florida. Mother gave him another chance at getting it right.

The day Stepfather arrived was a day of celebration, particularly for Mother. Everyone was thrilled to see him, and happy that he had made it without being caught by the authorities. He was happy to see us again—and, to my surprise, he was even happy to see me. Our previous relationship had been one of acceptance rather than admiration. He had never appeared to like me very much, and I didn't especially care for him. Even when he didn't speak of his dislike for me, his actions and facial expression had.

Seven of us were now living in my uncle's home. My brother and I had to move from the room we shared with Mother to our cousin's room; to make room for Stepfather. We were instantly replaced by his presence.

Although there were still laughter and joy, the good times never seemed to last for long. Stepfather's demeanor began to change, as before, he found fault in everything I did. Nothing I had done was as good as his precious daughter would have done it. He and Mother were falling back into their old familiar routines again, including their constant verbal combats.

Cousin Sam had also become a permanent fixture in Uncle's home; driving Stepfather around, helping him become acquainted with his new surroundings. He also took Stepfather to card games in the evenings. Stepfather made new friends and quickly became reacquainted with some old ones. His days were beginning to stretch into nights. His return to drinking and playing cards was imminent.

He had only been in Florida for a short time, but it felt like a lifetime had passed. Our lives were almost as chaotic as before. By now, Mother had given birth to her third child, another baby boy—my brother Jude. I was as excited to see him as I had felt when I saw Joshua. I still wanted him to be mine just as Joshua had been. When Mother came home from the hospital, and I saw Jude for the first time, it was a moment of blissful joy.

The day after Mother and the baby returned home, Stepfather expressed his dislikes for how dark the baby looked. He wanted to know why the baby didn't have his light complexion, why he wasn't as light as Joshua had been as a baby. Mother appeared irritated. She responded by simply telling him that he was married to a woman of dark complexion and that if he wanted all of the children to look like him, he should have married someone who had possessed his complexion. Mother told him that he shouldn't expect all the children to have his complexion. She told him that she couldn't favor one child over the other based on complexion, and that even his own daughter was her child, despite the fact that she had not given birth to her.

I was thrilled to hear Mother's response. I had never heard her speak so passionately about us before. I was happy that she seemed delighted to be our mother. It was at that moment that I felt she really loved use, loved me. Although now, I realized she showed her love in a different way. It was the way she had described us children in such an endearing way that made me feel all tingly inside. It was the way she so eloquently defended us, her babies, which made me feel in my heart that she had loved us all along.

Seeing the look on Stepfather face; looking at his new son, my brother in a way that was upsetting. At that moment I felt as if I needed to watch over the baby more carefully than I had been with Joshua. Mother was still very hurt by Stepfather's implication. It was the hurt in her eyes from his comments and the love in her heart that compelled me to think differently about my purpose and what it meant to be an older sister to my brothers. At that moment, I understood the true differences between our two complexions. I understood that my new baby brother and I were different. Because we shared the same complexion, I felt that I needed to protect him from Stepfather. Now I had a greater purpose for living—to protect my brothers from Stepfather's thoughtless remark.

XVI

A PLACE CALLED HOME

Mother and Stepfather returned to their former routines. The abuse didn't stop the way I had hoped. Only the people were different in a different place. I still had not been able to speak with anyone about the continued derailments of my innocence. Besides my baby brother, who was nearing his second birthday, the only other person I felt close to was my Auntie Angel. She was a very kind, loving, and nurturing woman.

We continued to live in Uncle Harry's home, but it was getting very crowded and the tensions between everyone just increased. Stepfather had been looking for work, and after several long months, he finally found a job. Mother and Stepfather hoped to save money from his new income to buy him a used car and to help get an apartment. Stepfather didn't want to remain in Uncle's home much longer. But the search for an apartment started sooner than planned.

I have never forgotten what propelled them to act so quickly. It was a normal day like any other, Mother had returned from work, and as was her routine, prepared my baby brother for his evening bath.

She removed his soiled diaper and placed it in the toilet bin, following the bath, Mother handed the baby to me to help with his feeding, as she handed the baby to me, Uncle Harry was walking in the door from his taxi job. His routine was always the toilet with his daily newspaper. However, this time when he came out of the toilet, he was holding the trash bin.

He walked over to where I sat feeding the baby, and without any question, poured the contents of the bin over my head, soiled diapers and all. He toke it a step further and shoved the bin down over my head. In complete horror and dismay, I abruptly stood to free my airways, and forgot that I had been feeding the baby. When I stood up, he fell to the ground. To this day, I can still hear the thumping sound his little body made when he hit the tile floor.

The baby let out a wailing cry and mother rushed into the dining room to see what had happened to make the baby cry so loudly. She saw me standing with the trash over my head and at my feet, she saw the baby on the floor and both of us were crying. I recall the expression of shock and anger on Mother's face. She instantly knew he had done it without me saying anything. Mother charged at him, but Uncle Harry quickly retreated to his bedroom. They exchanged harsh words through the door as Mother helped me clean up the mess and care for my brother. That evening, Mother cried and cried with anger. She swore that Uncle Harry would never get another chance to treat us as if we were dogs.

The following week, Mother and Stepfather found a small, furnished apartment and immediately moved. The apartment was very small, but it was ours. We could touch the walls if we stretched our arms far enough. For awhile at least, I felt safe. No one came around as much, but eventually they started playing cards in our home again on Friday nights. This time, it wasn't the need for money; it was more for the company and something to do. I hated that they were always coming in and out of our home just as they had done in the Caribbean—arriving unannounced and unexpected. I started living in constant fear again, always wondering about what might happen, who among their friends or our family who was going to hurt me again.

When we had lived at Uncle Harry's, Cousin Sam had started doing the same things that Uncle Gabe had done to me many times. He would offer to watch us whenever Mother needed someone or when Auntie Angel was not available. He would volunteer his time, because he was touching me repeatedly. I would protest, but he never cared.

It was dreadful reliving those horrible nightmares all over again. I hated the way he looked at me. He would make these disgusting gestures, licking his lips slowly with his tongue. He would try touching parts of my body—my legs or my thighs. When my younger cousins and I would play outside in the yard, he would find an excuse to make me come back into the house; always under the pretence of wanting me to do something; asking me to get him water or food, or pretend that the baby was crying.

He would try getting me to be alone with him. He would touch me and I would pretend that I was someone else— another girl that he was doing those things. I would blame myself, because the outcomes were always the same. I despised him just as I had detested Uncle Gabe. I despised myself for being so unlucky. I didn't want to believe this was happening repeated. I felt as if I had been cursed, so I never talked about it. I kept all of the details to myself; all their dirty secrets were my burden to carry.

Cousin Sam repulsed me; he always smelled like days-old cigarettes and alcohol mixed together. His mouth always smelled disgusting with his stained yellow teeth. He smoked incessantly. During his acts against me, he would try putting his mouth on me. He would try holding my face; trying to force my mouth open. I would push him, and try moving my face away, wanting to vomit.

I have not escaped those images. I remember once I tried to bite him so he would let go, but he responded by hitting me. After each violation, he would try to give me money for the ice cream truck. He would try to buy my silence just as Uncle Gabe had done.

Afterwards, I would feel unclean. I would run to the shower to wash off his smell that seemed to linger on my skin. I couldn't take enough showers; there was never enough soap to wash away how dirty I felt. While in the shower, I would scrub my body, my skin, my face, and my private area. My skin would burn from rubbing so hard and from using the green rubbing alcohol to kill his germs.

I was afraid of telling anyone about my ordeal, mostly because I feared Mother would send me back to Haiti—that had always been the threat. As awful as the situation was, I much preferred to be with Mother and my brothers. I thought that if I told her what had been happening, I would be blamed. They would say that it was my fault. They would think I was a bad and dirty girl.

One time, he nearly got caught doing those nasty things to me; I was nearly freed from carrying the secrets of his constant violation. It was Auntie Angel who nearly caught him. One day, as he waited for Auntie Angel to get home from work, he was doing what he had always done, putting his hand under my dress while I was trying to do my schoolwork at the dining table.

That day, Auntie arrived home much earlier than expected. We were both sitting at the table while he ate, and while I was trying to do my schoolwork. Whenever he came around, he would sit facing the glass sliding door leading to the carport, the door that was used most often. Auntie Angel walked into the house just as I was crying because he wouldn't leave me alone. When he saw Auntie Angel, he quickly removed his hand. Auntie Angel wanted to know why I was crying, but I couldn't tell her; even if I wanted to, before I could think of what to say, he told Auntie Angel that he spanked me for being disrespectful to him. Instantly, my tears were justified and he seemed justified with his explanation.

I remained silent about their dirty deeds. Just as Uncle Gabe had warned me not to tell anyone, Cousin Sam likewise said no one would believe me, and just as before, I listened. Besides, he was the adult and I was the child. In our home, children obeyed whatever they were told to do by the adults. I had lived with so much fear and guilt for believing that their actions had been my fault. I came to believe that it was normal and natural for older men to do things to little girls.

So many times, I wanted to kill myself just to get away. I thought a lot about death, how I would do it, what I would use. The only suicide "tool" I had heard or knew about was battery acid. I thought about drinking the acid, or stabbing myself with a knife, but the more I thought about it, the more I knew I couldn't take my own life.

I couldn't do it no matter how bad the situations were. I felt that if I ended my own life, I would go to hell. I would also do a grave injustice to my brothers. For a long time, I thought and accepted that

I was a foolish coward, afraid of my own blood, and afraid of my own death. I thought about my friend Yannic who had died so young, and I knew that I didn't want to die as young. I just wanted to make them stop.

I thought about my brothers, I wondered who would care for them if I died. I thought about the promise I made to protect them for as long as I was able. But many, many nights, I labored over the thought of dying, but it seemed too easy of a choice. I knew and believed deep in my heart that those men who were causing me pain were not worth my life.

The older I got, the more withdrawn I became. It was as if I had become immune to their abuse. I didn't care about what they did to me anymore, because they had ignored my protests and had threatened me with bodily harm or deportation. Although the abuse wasn't occurring as frequently anymore, I felt that I didn't have anything left for anyone new or old to take.

They had taken all that I had been told had made me pure. Now I was soiled, they had taken the sacred part of what I understood would make me special, worthy, and untainted. I just wanted to break free.

I wanted to show and prove to them that I was strong. With God and prayer, I would withstand whatever they had done and whatever they would continue to do to me. I envisioned that, one day, they would pay for what they had done. I wanted so much to be a witness to that time when they would pay. I wanted to prove to them that I would become somebody someday for myself and for my brothers. My brothers had fueled my determination to live. I felt that even in death, I wouldn't be able to forgive myself for giving up on them, knowing I had taken the easy way out.

XVII

AN UNLIKELY FATHER

So much had happened in such a short time. By then, I was thirteen years old and felt that I had lived way beyond my years. We had moved from the apartment into a white wooden house. Also by then, Stepsister had joined us again after being separated for what seemed like an eternity. When I saw Stepsister since nearly two years, she appeared more grown up than I remembered. She seemed different, in much of the way I've felt different

    The feelings I had when we were together in the Caribbean had remained the same--disconnected. I still felt small in her presence, and as before, everyone embraced her. I still had to listen to everyone tell her how much prettier she was to me, while they ridiculed my darkness. Those constant comparisons really drove a wedge between us. Although the way I had been received was no fault of hers, I felt resentful of always feeling second best; and although our interactions have remained friendly and cordial over the years. I've shielded and protected any feelings towards her. I didn't know how to embrace her without feeling inferior, so I kept my distance.

Things were back to how they once were. Stepfather made me feel less than invisible. He never noticed me until he needed something doing—to get his food or wash his sweaty blistered toes. I resented Stepfather for not caring, for never truly embracing and accepting my dark-skinned brother.

I would have given my soul, if I thought it would have made life better for all of us.

Over time, a new group of immigrants were emerging at our home. Our home seemed to be the place where they would all come to; to become acquainted with one another. It was always the same old routine. Although, Mother had been a force to reckoned with, her compelling trust of others had blinded her to what was going on in her own home. Stepfather was no more present than she had been. They were drifters, going from work to playing cards, and we were practically left to raise ourselves; but the fear they imposed on us, was enough to keep us on the straight and narrow.

Life was not always as chaotic, there were the few occasions I can remember the good times, particularly on a Friday or Saturday night when their favorite bands were in town. They would dress us up and take us with them to the ball dance. Those events were great social outlets for many families. I enjoyed going to the ball dances, there I felt free and pretty in my pretty dresses and new shoes Mother would buy us, just so we would make our appearance and I would dance my little heart to exhaustion. On the dance floor, I would dance with Stepfather, he was like a different person when he was dancing, the only time he ever complemented me was when I danced with him. He always thought I was a good dancer, he said that I was light on my feet, when he had to twirl me around.

The truth of the matter is, both Mother and Stepfather tried very hard to keep the vultures away and provide a good home, but they circumstances were challenging. My experience of momentary order came from my Uncle Benny.

I was grateful that Uncle Benny came into my life when he did. His presence made me feel hopeful. Known as easily excitable, Uncle Benny influenced the actions of the men who played cards at our home. They seemed to behave differently when he was around, and he was at our home as frequently as the vultures. It was like he was my personal bodyguard. I felt protected. For the first time in my life, someone connected with my need to feel safe. He offered that safety blanket, even though he was unaware of how much I needed his protection. My Uncle Benny became that protective male presence I needed, and the fatherly authority I had not had since my father and I parted ways that day at the boating dock. Uncle Benny was the fatherly presence that Stepfather never provided was able to be.

The changes in our home were subtle, but enough to make an impact. It was as if Uncle Benny could sniff out the vultures lurking in our home. On his many visits, he would jokingly (or seemingly so) tell the men that he had better not catch them with their hands on either Stepsister or me.

Even today I can hardly describe the feelings of the temporary empowerment I felt. He didn't allow Stepsister or me to linger around as before to fetch food and water for the card players. Mother or someone else had to serve them. If we had chores to do while those vultures were in our home, he made sure we did them at rapid speed or at a time when the vultures weren't around. Uncle Benny was a beam of light in my life that had once been overshadowed by darkness. He was an element of order, however temporary.

Life was slowly turning around, except that the nonexistent relationship between Mother and me continued to decline further into an abyss. Every day, I grew angrier at Mother. I blamed her for all the disappointments and the shame I had experienced. I blamed her for not protecting me, for not being aware of the damages that her so-called friend were causing; for not being available to my brothers and me.

"Home" represented many darkness and shadowy days, and I hated being there. It never felt like a home, more of a temporary shelter—a place to pass time, rather than a place of comfort, nourishment, or love. It was never a part of me, nor did it instill a feeling of belonging. For many years, I contemplated running away, but I didn't know where I would go. I didn't have any money and I couldn't muster the nerve to fight back, so I stayed and endured whatever came my way.

I never felt comfortable being there—not in the home, and not in my own skin. I was desperate for a solution outside of my uncle's temporary protection. I wanted to fight back but was afraid of the outcome. I knew I had to think of a plan to change the situation at home. I had learned at school that playing cards for money was illegal and I wanted to report the games. But after thinking about my brothers, I couldn't bring myself to call the authorities. I was afraid of what would happen to us. I didn't want to hurt Mother or Stepfather. I just wanted the people to stop coming to our home. I was living in fear of what would happen to me if they continued coming around.

Although, Uncle Benny was a good deterrent, he couldn't undo the past. He couldn't make my feelings of wanting to kill myself go away. Many times, I thought about picking up the telephone to reporting everything, but I was afraid, wondering where we would go. If people would criticize us, or even understand our culture, would they say unkind remarks; or be placed somewhere that would be much worse than home. I was afraid of Mother and Stepfather's reactions if they found out that I had called the authorities. I thought about the kind of problems I would create for them and for myself. The trouble I would face with the family and our small community.

In my culture, children didn't rebel or retaliate against their parents. In my community, it was taboo for children to talk back, disobey, disappoint, or shame our parents and families. Going against the rules would have brought great shame upon my family. I didn't want to think about what they would do, or how bad the beatings would be. I didn't want to be the person to hurt Mother because I knew she was trying her best to do whatever she needed to do to care for us. Perhaps I didn't understand the sacrifices she was making so that our family wouldn't have to live in the so-called projects, the broken up apartments.

I wanted to leave, but not without my brothers. I didn't want to be the source of blame if something bad happened to them. I didn't want any harm to come to them, and I didn't want it to be my fault.

Life was spiraling into hell. We had moved to a larger apartment, and although Mother and Stepfather were making a real effort to ensure life was better for us by not allowing as many card games as before, the damages to me personally had already been done. I no longer cared about their renewed efforts to protect and shelter us from their friends.

As far as I was concerned, they were five years too late. I had given up caring or fighting. The punishments they inflicted on me five years earlier seemed commonplace.

I believed that most men, if not all of them, did such things to young girls. I also believed that if anyone wanted to hurt me again, they would find a way and I would have no control over the situation, no control over what they would do, or if I would be able to stop them.

XVIII

THE SILVER LINNING

Although life seemed to be getting better, the shame of my situation never escaped me. My life had become my own secret, and unless someone already knew about it the card playing, they would not have learned it from me. I refused to have friends visit my home, because I didn't want them to see what my home life was like. I didn't want to justify my family's actions to anyone.

School was the one place where I could escape my situation. Even though I wanted the pain to stop, I was afraid that people from outside of our community wouldn't understand. They wouldn't understand that my mother and Stepfather were doing their best, and perhaps they would not want to speak to me. Maybe other parents wouldn't want their children to befriend me, or worse, they might report us. As much as I wanted to escape it all, I didn't want to be the cause of Mother and Stepfather's troubles.

For awhile, I wanted to believe that I was happy, but the happy times never lasted. Mother had taken to beating me and most of the times I was on the receiving end of her frustrations, and the brunt of her anger. I was constantly walking on broken glasses, trying my best to stay out of her way, trying to avoid detection. Everything I did was to please her. I hoped to be in her favor, and to be invisible to her constant anger. My efforts to please her didn't seem to help much. I endured occasional spankings, name-calling episodes, and even a few slaps now and again, but the beatings had become more ferocious.

Her angers seemed directed towards me; because I felt that she treated my brothers and my stepsister differently. I felt perhaps the reason was partly because my father wasn't around for me like Stepfather was for his children. I felt I was paying for what Father had done or had not done. I wondered if she felt burdened by me, an extra mouth to feed, and an extra body to clothe with no apparent help from my father.

Life felt like a block of concrete, heavy and gray and the only rays of sunshine in my life were my brothers and knowing that Mother was expecting another baby, which would now be her fifth child including Stepsister. She was having another little person for me to care for, I thought maybe with another baby in our home, things would be different; at least temporarily, I would be happy again. I was hoping that Mother's pregnancy would change her and Stepfather's relationship.

I suppose the constant nagging of never feeling wanted or good enough has made me feel like running away, just to look for that better life somewhere else. Running away had not really been an option, although I always thought about it, I was so afraid of disobeying and disappointing Mother, Father, and the family. I didn't want to give Stepfather anymore reasons to further dislike or disapprove of me. I was afraid he would think I was such a bad influence on his precious daughter and sons.

But things were so bad that one day, despite my fears, I made up my mind to leave, run away, even if it meant I would probably have to live on the streets. I knew that my aunts and uncles wouldn't take me in their homes. My family would understand, maybe even shun me for leaving Mother's home. To them, running away from home was a sure sign of defiance. Families and friends would be forbidden to speak to or help me. They would automatically assume that I had ran away because I wanted to be slack and independent—so I could force my adulthood earlier.

The actions that set the paste for me, and deciding to risk the ostracizing was the day I remember Mother coming from the immigrations office. That morning, she had gone there to see about getting our green cards so we could become legal immigrants. Before leaving, Mother prepared a pot of meat to cook for dinner. She had instructed me to watch over it while it cooked slowly on the stove. Before she left, she added just enough water for it to simmer and so that I wouldn't have to continue adding water to it. I did as she asked and occasionally checked the level of the liquid.

Over the time I checked on the pot, I hadn't notice that the large pot of meat was getting smaller. I thought it was natural for it to shrink as it cooked. I was unaware one of my mother's friend daughter who was staying with us at the time had been eating the meat as it cooked on the stove.

Upon returning, Mother checked the stove and found that the once full pot of freshly seasoned meat had been reduced to half. The girl had eaten half the meat! When Mother asked what happened, I couldn't tell her. She had left me in charge; therefore, it was my responsibility to keep and eye on the meat and prevent anyone from eating it before dinner.

Mother went to her room to find a belt and began beating me. My mistake was in trying to hold the belt. Mother then reached for the umbrella on the table and repeatedly slammed it against my body. She swung it, hitting whatever part of my body the umbrella landed on. Then came the final blow; Mother whacked me across my throat with the umbrella, at that moment, I felt as though she was trying to kill me.

None of the previous beatings had been as horrible as that one. I was badly scratched and bruised. Days later, I was still in pain and was unable to swallow properly. My swollen neck seemed to get worse as time went on, so much so that eventually Mother toke me to the doctors. I couldn't tell the doctor, that my mother had beaten me with an umbrella that caused my neck to swell. After all, who would believe me? The doctor diagnosed an enlarged thyroid and said I might require surgery to remove it.

He sent me home with a prescription to reduce the swelling. But In my heart, I believed my swollen neck was the result of Mother's beating, and not thyroid, so I refused to take the pills.

XIX

RUNAWAY

The plans and contemplation to run away were in motion. I had heard discussions about my *grandmère* and sister that they were now living in Florida as well. I did not care where they were, I was determined to get to them both. I wanted to tell them why I wanted to leave home—because of the beatings and the men who were hurting me. I thought that perhaps they would tell my father, and he, in turn, would let me live with them. I prayed that my father would want to take care of me and that he'd believe me when I told him about what the men had done.

The situation at home was unbearable. I had planned my escape. One morning at about five o'clock in the morning, I woke up while everyone was still sleeping, filled a small trash bag with a few of my belongings and left Mother's home and headed to Ms. Marco's home—the woman I had met in Haiti and in the Caribbean with my grandmother—the mother of my brothers and sister. They now lived only several long blocks from our home. My brothers, sister and I had visited each other's homes before, since our chance meeting at the nearby school we all attended. They had become my family again.

I was very scared as I walked alone in the darkness. I was afraid someone might attack me. Despite my fears, I was determined to get there. I walked swiftly, glancing over my shoulders, and wondering if I would make it to their home before Mother realized I was gone. When I heard any noise or saw any car coming in my direction, I would run for cover and hide behind the nearest bush I found, until I was alone again. I finally reached my brother's and sister's home and knocked on their bedroom window. They were surprised to see me standing there with my black trash bag, with tears streaming down my cheeks.

Without their mother's knowledge, they let me into the house through the kitchen door. I remember sitting with them, together, contemplated my next move. Wondering how I would get to *grandmère's* home. I told them that I was running away because I had been mistreated—but nothing else. As I sat there, crying, wanting to die. I felt that this was my last effort to get away, I was desperate. I didn't care what Mother would do, even if she decided to send me back to Haiti. I was determined to leave.

My brothers and sister hid me in their bedroom closet so their mother's wouldn't see me when she came in to wake them up for school. I told them that I wanted to find our *grandmère* so that I can live with her, to be safe; even if it meant that I might die trying; at least I would be free.

I was afraid of what Mother would do when she discovered I was gone. Part of me wanted to see the surprised look on her face; another part of me was scared of her real reaction—her true anger. I imagined that she would put her arms around me, apologizing for mistreating me. Then I would embrace her, and tell her that I loved her still and would forgive her. I fantasized that she would tell me she loved me and wanted me back home. But the reality wasn't anything like my fantasies.

I learned that when Mother awoke for work that morning and discovered I wasn't in my bed and had gone, her reaction wasn't one of sympathy. She was furious.

It was as if she had known that I ran away. Early that morning I heard my brothers and sisters telephone ring. It was mother; she was calling the only place she thought I might have gone to. As I crouched in the closet, I heard the conversation between their mother and mine. Ms. Marco telling Mother that she had not seen me and that I wasn't in her home.

Little did she know that I was hiding in her closet all along! As Mother and Ms. Marco continued their conversation, my brothers, sister and I were forming a plan. One of the four boys suggested that their mothers be informed that I was hiding in the closet and tell her the whole story in the hope that she would help me.

Collectively, the six of us agreed to tell Ms. Marco that I had been hiding in her home; but the outcome wasn't what we had anticipated. She was surprised to learn that I had been in the closet during her telephone conversation with Mother. All of us tried to convince her not to call Mother, but she said it was best that she did, because Mother was worried sick. She needed to let Mother know that she had found me and I was in her home.

Ms. Marco tried her best to assure me that everything would be okay; all I thought about was how Mother was going to react, how she would kill me. I cried and pleaded for her to help me get to my *grandmère's* home. No one was prepared to deal with my mother's wrath.

Shortly after calling Mother with the news, she and one of my cousins arrived at Ms. Marco's home. When she walked through the front door with her very pregnant frame, I was trembling. I felt like I had gone insane, I felt like a trapped animal. I remember feeling the wet, hot urine trickled down my legs from anxiety, yet I was determined to break free. My eighty-pound frame stood firm against Mother's stronger, more determined posture.

Mother instructed me to get my things so we would leave, but my mouth exploded. I couldn't stop the words from escaping my mouth. I told Mother that I would only leave with the police or in a body bag.

I told her that I didn't want to live with her anymore. I remember as soon as spoke those words out of my mouth, Mother swung her arm and knocked me against the wall. She was furious, and even though she was very pregnant, she still lunged at me; trying to grab me. That day my brothers had become my heroes. As young as they were, even with their mothers looking on, they lined up in front of me, as determined as I was, not to let me go.

Mother tried pulling me out of their home and they were pulling back. Their mothers pleaded with me to leave peacefully, so that I wouldn't make matters worse when I got back home. She didn't realize that several events had already taken very drastic turns; and that moment was as good as it was going to get.

During the struggle, I broke free from my mother's grip and tried making a run for the kitchen so I can escape out the back door.

However, my cousin grabbed hold of me and carried me out to his car.

I remember on the drive back to our home, Mother turned towards the back seat and continued hitting me with her slipper and her hand. After we got home, she dragged me into the bedroom and whipped me as if her very life depended on it.

For as long as I can remember, whenever I got a beating, I would urinate on myself, and that day was no different. In fact, I left several puddles on the ground that day; there was plenty of water to go around.

Mother continued doing what she always did best. She gave it to me real good. The blows from the belt were coming in all directions. I knelt and shielded my face in defense, because she was hitting like a whirlwind. I wanted to prevent the swinging belt buckle from hitting or cutting my face. Mother was in a rage, she didn't particularly care where the belt or any other object she lashed out at me landed. The mistakes I always made, was trying to force her to stop by holding on whatever she was using to whip me with at that time.

Again, in a moment of my own insanity, I attempted to grab hold of the belt from her, which only made her angrier. As usual, whenever I would try to get her to stop, she would always think that I was trying to fight her back or was being disrespectful. She was furious that I had the audacity to stand up to her; and where the belt couldn't reach, or when her arms were tired, her feet managed to complete. That morning, after mother finished, as she left for work, she instructed various families to watch me, making sure that I wouldn't try to escape again.

XX
BEWILDERED

When I looked in the mirror at my swollen face and bruised body; looking for any cuts, there were no visible cuts, just welts. The dismay in my eyes as I looked in that mirror left me wondering what else Mother would do. I prayed the ordeal would be over by the time she returned home from work. I wanted to get through the day and not think anymore of what had happened.

Mother, however, had not forgotten. When she returned home from work that evening, she wanted to make sure that I had eaten. She prepared dinner and served to me, all the while fussing about my audacity for trying to run away from her home. Her justification was that she had brought me into the world and would take me out if she wanted to and she seemed angrier than she had been that morning.

While I was trying to work up an appetite to eat what she had prepared for me, still whimpering at the table, my brothers were teasing me about the beating. When I asked them to stop and leave me alone, Mother became upset again, accusing me of hitting one of the boys.

Then there was a few more slaps, because I shouldn't have asked them to stop.

In spite of Mother's anger, one thing that was always certain in our home after every thrashing; the request would always be the same, a nice cold bath to soothe the bruises and a nice meal to top the occasion, or depending on the time of day, a nice bowl of banana pourage and buttered bread would be the comfort.

Mother wanted to see to it that my body replenished the energy and strength lost from the exertion of crying, not to forget the freshly grated beets and carrot juices she would make. But later that night, before going to bed, Mother made me a fresh cup of ginger tea to help ease my pain, and burnt sour orange with salt and oil to apply to my bruised arms.

For a long time, I suppressed the angers I felt. Sadness and torment became my way of life. I was angry with Mother for not loving me enough, at Father for not being around for me, and furious with myself for thinking that running away would solve my problems. Instead, it had made things worse. I couldn't see past the hurt. My love and admiration for Mother turned to fear and loathing.

XXI

IN SEARCH OF HARMONY

I've lost myself in my own fantasies, wondering if others lived as I did—constantly fearful, vulnerable, and feeling out of control. My most peaceful moments were spent at school, which allowed me some freedom I never had at home. At school, I felt as if I were living in another world. Mother was overly protective and didn't allow me to make many friends without her approval.

I would try to minimizing the frictions by being passive and accepting of everything. With Stepsister, communication was minimal. Even though she and I were of same age, just shy of a week, I felt that I had nothing in common with her. I couldn't get over how everyone made me feel when she was present.

My relationship with her had always been one of tolerance and as life evolved; my brothers had become my only true companions.

Outside of our immediate home; I enjoyed spending time with my other brothers and sisters. Wanting so much to feel normal, to have

Fragments of a Fractured Life

friends outside of my family and siblings, but mother was uncomfortable relinquishing her control.

Over time, I met a girl who lived across the street from our home. Occasionally on the weekends, after our chores were done, Mother would allow Stepsister and me to play with her, and gradually, she and I became good friends. Her name was Monique. Our friendship didn't last very long, though, because Mother had learned that Monique's sister had given birth to a child at a very young age.

Mother forbade me from playing with Monique; she said that if I continued playing with her, her sister would influence my behavior. She told me that I would be judged by the company I kept, and that she wouldn't allow anyone to think that I would follow a similar path.

Under Mother's control and watchful eye, my friendship with Monique slowly dissolved. I was sad that I had to say good-bye to my friend, and sad that Mother forbade me to speak with her for what her sister had done. Monique and I were cordial with each other; things were never again the same between us. I had never felt so empty and confused; trying to understand Mother's control.

I suppose, she wanted to make sure that I did not mess up my life by being with the wrong crowd. Just as I was getting over my friendship with Monique, another girl in our neighborhood entered my life.

She was someone I thought might meet Mother's approval. She would occasionally stroll by our home on errands. I remember when I saw her; how very pretty I thought she was, unlike Stepsister and me. I imagined that, at her home, her family treated her as special. From a distance, I admired her because she had the freedom to do as she pleased. She appeared not to have a care in the world.

She would take the same shortcut—along the side road facing our kitchen—she would go back and forth between the supermarket and Laundromat. I would watch her go by from our dining room window, wondering if I would ever be as free as she seemed, able to roam without restrictions or limitations.

I envied her space and freedom. I would wonder if we could ever be friends or would she want to. I was putting up the barriers before Mother had a chance to. I had already told myself that I was inferior to her seamless beauty. I wondered if her mother was like my mother, if she was nicer, and gentler.

On a chance day, we met at the market by chance. Yet, in a way, the meeting was predictable, because we routinely walked home from school on the same road. I remember that she introduced herself and asked my name. I hesitated; I was afraid of what Mother would say. For a quick moment, I lowered that protective shield of Mother's and told her my name. Her name was easy to remember, yet I repeated it in my mind, not wanting to forget it. That day, we walked home awkwardly talking about nothing at all. It was the start of a slow brewing friendship, but over time, it became apparent how much her friendship meant to me.

I was entering tenth grade, but Mother could not afford to continue paying for my private education. I decided that I would attend public in another city, a much better public school with few distractions. It was during our morning walks to the bus stop that our friendship evolved, particularly after our mothers met. The two women seemed to know each other, the way they were talking the first time they met. Mother didn't seem to mind that I knew Solange, but she wanted to know if she was a good girl.

Every morning thereafter, our mothers took turns walking us to the bus stop. The first time Mother walked with us, Solange was surprised to see that she carried her machete—in case someone decided to jump out from the bushes or intended attack or rob us. Walking to the bus stop in the morning was an adventure for and I believe Solange, because we never knew what our mothers would say or do. They were funny together; Mother was becoming more relaxed than before.

School was exciting as well as challenging; especially when it came to dealing with the girl's. Usually they would tease, calling Solange and me "Sunshine" and "Midnight," the "proper girls," or "white girls in black skin." They accused us of speaking too proper or not being "black enough." That school was quite different from my previous Catholic school, but it I still liked the excitement and the escape it offered. I was making new friends and life was good.

I liked the school, particularly because it was farther away from my home. I enjoyed the long ride home on the bus. I had a sense of freedom I never felt before; where I could be myself. It was during those long bus rides and walks home that our friendship truly developed. I envied Solange for the things that I wasn't. I admired her liveliness. I lived through her friendship; I thought of her more like a sister than a friend, similar to my own sister Marsha and certainly more than Stepsister had been.

On weekends Mother would allow me to go out with my friends, as long as I was back home by ten o'clock, and sometimes when she was feeling a little generous she would allow me to stay out until eleven. Other times she would allow me to stay out later if I was with my Uncle Benny. He would take us out to eat and to the clubs, I was always happy to have my Uncle Benny in my corner.

XXII

BORDERLINE

Since graduating from High School, life had newer meaning, and since I was approaching my twentieth birthday, the past still lingered in my mind, but one thought continued to puzzle me—that I might still be a virgin even after all those years of abuse. The thoughts began to invade my mind after I had overheard a strange conversation about what happened when women loses their virginity.

I had heard that a woman would bleed like a slaughtered goat on the sheets, the first time. I also heard about other things that would happen to her body. From those conversations, I had the crazy notion in my head that, perhaps, I was unbroken. I recalled all the words my abusers had used each time they violated me. They told me that they wouldn't make me bleed. For whatever reason, just thinking about those words gave me a glimmer of hope I might still be okay.

I wanted so much to believe that what they had said were true. If nothing else, I wanted to find out for myself if I was still intact. I had lived with the shame of possibly ever finding someone who would respect me if he learned what happened to me—if he learned that I wasn't a virgin. Although, I had given up all hopes and knew in my heart that I could not reversing what they had done, I was on a mission to find out how far they had gone, how deeply they had damaged my development.

I constantly thought of my violators' comments—how they didn't want Mother to know. I remembered the words Uncle Gabe whispered, "I won't make you bleed." My curiosity about whether I was a virgin weighed heavily on my mind. I wanted to know if there was any possibility that I had not been physically broken inside, although the emotional scars were much more painful than I can ever express.

I feared I would be worthless to any man who would want to marry me. Mother told me that a husband respects his wife more if she saved herself him until marriage. But I gave up the thought of receiving such admiration from any man. I didn't want to continue living under false pretenses—the fantasy that I was pure, a virgin. They had taken that privilege from me. They deprived me of such magnificent glory.

I felt unsettled, and uncertain of the future. I wanted to be free of my doubts, I was determined to uncover my own truth about whether or not I was still a virgin or if I should continue to live the fantasy of wanting to be one until I married.

I decided that for my twentieth birthday, I would do things my way. I wanted to find out for myself, before marriage, if I was severely damaged. I set out to give myself to someone of my choosing. I wanted to find out if my seal had been broken--as Mother would say.

The next step to my plan was to find a person worthy of going through this troubling discovery with me. I wanted this decision to be one of my proudest moments, and whatever happens; I wanted it to be the result of my own freewill. Since overhearing the conversation between those women, I held on to the thoughts that I might be able to regain some of my dignity. Although, I had been fractured in many ways, and in many places, perhaps I wasn't completely broken.

My birthday was rapidly approaching with no possible partner in sight. Then I met Serge; I wanted him to be the chosen one—the one to "unseal my envelope," I wanted the day to be very special for both of us. He was handsome; well dressed and well spoken. He was tall, debonair, and had the most beautiful smiling eyes I had ever seen.

My biggest challenge was deciding on the perfect time to speak to him. I pursued him as much as he pursued me, and after weeks of idle conversation, the plan was fully set in motion.

Serge's seductive eyes and beautiful flirtatious smile made it all too easy. I wanted to prove to myself and to everyone else who had belittled me that someone like him could be attracted to me.

The first time I saw him or met him was in front of the trade school I was attending at night for typing. He was standing in a crowd of young women who were admiring him as much as I was. He looked over in my direction and our eyes met, and shortly thereafter, he walked over and say hello to my friends and me.

We flirted from the start, and by the end of our conversation, he had given me his telephone number. Talking to him confirmed my thoughts. I wanted him to be my first true experience.

We spoke constantly; and after several conversations over the telephone and a few lunches and dinners, I told him that it was my birthday wish to have him b e my first love. From his response, I could tell he was excited about being the one with the experiences. During the next month, the anticipation leading up to the day became overwhelming. I thought about the outcome and wondered what Mother would say, but I just didn't care about that anymore. I was determined to take control of my own thoughts, my decisions, and my life.

I thought about all the bragging he had done about being a good lover—I couldn't tell you who would a good lover or not, and how experienced he was. Even though those conversations left me feeling embarrassed off putting, I wanted to appear mature to him and impress him in every way. I wondered if he would be true to his words—caring, loving, and gentle or if I would measure up to his expectations. What I knew about love and passion I had learned from watching soap operas on television. On our special day, I wanted Serge and me to be as happy as those people had been. I was anxious to know if I was unbroken, and I wanted to feel that someone cared for and loved me.

I wanted to know if he would be honored to be with me, knowing that I was a virgin and waiting to give myself to him, or if he would be disappointed that I was tainted. I found myself drifting to Stepsister to ask about her experiences, without going into much detail. We talked about her experiences with her boyfriends. She described them as "moving mountains." I wanted to feel the mountains move for me, too. I wanted Serge to hold me in his arms and tell me how special I was, as Stepsister's boyfriends had told her.

On the special day, we met at a nearby hotel overlooking the ocean. He was waiting for me on the second level. I climbed the stairs. My head was heavy with the weight of anticipation. We met in front of the room and together walked into it. Both of us sat at the foot of the bed like two lost kids. My heart was beating like wild drums, and my knees shook like Haitian ceremonial maracas. I wondered if this was how I was supposed to feel—scared, anxious, and excited all at the same time. I was frightened of the closeness and intensity between us. I felt as if the room were spinning out of control.

Before the ordeal had even started, I wanted it to be over. I had imagined the moment between us would be gentle. I wanted him to be. I felt the perspiration trickling from under my arms and down the side of my face, and the intense heat rising to my head. Suddenly he reached over and gently kissed my lips, and I was lost in the moment. That was the closest I had ever been with someone who had not forced me to be with him. Although I expected something to happen, I was surprised how much I wanted him to stop. My mind sent me mixed signals, yet I wanted him to like me. I didn't anticipate wanting to leave. I had committed my heart and myself. I needed to meet his expectations. He slowly unbuttoned my shirt and gently cupped my breasts. Then it happened. I felt a great deal of discomfort, but it was the gasping sound that he made that left me feeling cold— like a block of ice. As quickly as it had begun, it was over.

Mountains didn't move for me. There was no talking between us after the act, and I didn't have time to savor the experience. Instead, at the forefront of my mind were the images of the men who had violated me before, and my thoughts were still being violated, even during the most special of moments. I felt dirty, cheap, unclean, and violated all over again. Only this time, it was of my own doing. The experience wasn't anything as I had been told it would be, and certainly not as I had hoped. I felt deceived and wondered why any woman would subject herself to being used as a toilet.

After it was all over, he asked if I was pleased, if it was what I expected. All I could do was smile ever so slightly, as not to upset him. I didn't want him that the experience wasn't as he described it would be. He rolled out of the bed and headed to the shower, neither of us spoke. I wanted to ask him if I had missed something. I wanted to ask him if I should expect something else. I wanted to scream, but instead, I quietly whimpered. One thing was certain, he could never accuse me of not being a virgin because under me, on the white hotel sheets, were smears of red, not in the quantity described before—not like a slaughtered goat, but enough to confirm that I had remained sealed up until that moment with him. I had surrendered to my desire to find out the dreaded truth or untruth, now his task was complete.

From that moment, nothing Mother or anyone could have done would have taken away my joy of knowing that I was free. I didn't care if anyone found out that, at twenty, that I was no longer a virgin before marriage. I didn't care how bad the beatings would be if Mother found out about my rendezvous with a man I barely knew for a chance in finding my truth. I didn't care if I walked funny from the experience, as many said would be the case. All I cared about at that moment was that in my heart was that I had made my own choice.

That day, I reclaimed some of my dignity, no matter how brief. I did it on my terms and in my own way.

XXIII

AFFECTIONATE COMPOSURE

Meeting Rodrigue was one of the best things that had happened to me in the two years since Serge. He entered my life when I was still trying to assert my independence from Mother while resisting her control. He was a welcomed distraction to my otherwise drab and boring existence. He was full of excitement and daring. He was everything I wasn't. We were true opposites. I admired that he was outspoken and full of fire, and he wasn't afraid to let anyone know how he felt. Looking at the events that unfolded, I saw him as someone who would help me get through all the chaos that had been a part of my life. He made me feel special and beautiful.

Our relationship unfolded very suddenly and the attraction between us was very strong. I was getting over a two-year secret relationship and wasn't looking to be with anyone. I felt I was better being alone, but it all happened so unexpectedly. He seemed very different, and he knew a lot about many things—things I knew nothing about. I was impressed with how much he knew on any subject compared to how little I knew. He offered me a new insight on the world. We spoke on a completely different level than I had been able to do with anyone else. He challenged my mind and dared me to be unique. I believed that he had a very genuine and kind spirit that no one else saw. We were able to be vulnerable with one another.

We had met at his uncle's medical practice. Dr. G. had been our family's physician since moving to the community, and this was the first time I had seen him at the practice. On that particular day, I had driven to the clinic for an appointment. When I pulled into the parking space next to the clinic, in front of the Laundromat, Rodrigue was standing outside the clinic talking. When I stepped out of my car and headed toward the clinic, as I walked past him, I noticed he was watching me. Before I had a chance to reach the door, he held it open for me. I remember that he wore gray trousers and a long-sleeved powder-pink shirt. He smiled at me as I entered and I smiled back. I wrote my name on the chart and sat down. He had entered the back of the clinic and was standing behind the glass partition. He glanced at the chart after I had signed in, looked in my direction, and smiled again. As he gazed at me, I smiled at him. I felt a bit uneasy that he took such an interest in me, yet I felt flattered that he would take such an interest. He had a warm smile and seemed very charming. He certainly left an impression.

As I left the clinic after my visit, he followed me outside and asked my name. I was smitten but hesitated slightly, although he already knew my name. I felt obliged to tell him again, and not appear as if I were playing hard to get.

We talked for what seemed like hours, and he asked me very directly if I had a boyfriend. I was too happy to tell him that I didn't have one. He smiled broadly as if he had won the biggest prize and asked about my plans for the rest of the afternoon. I was in no hurry to be anywhere. I had already expected to spend the rest of my afternoon at the mall. We continued talking outside the clinic about nothing at all, yet everything. I learned that he was visiting from Boston. He told me that he was related to the doctor and was working at the clinic to earn money for a car.

He was pleasant, polite, and very well mannered. When it was time for me to leave, he suggested that he accompany me to the mall. Although I thought he was quite forward, I agreed. On the way there, a connection was forming between us. He seemed very forthcoming with information. He never ran out of things to say. By the time we reached the mall, I had learned so much about him and his family. I didn't think there was anything else that he hadn't told me.

When I drove him back to the clinic that evening, he gave me his telephone number. I couldn't give him my number because, even at my age of twenty-two, Mother didn't want or like any male figures calling on me unless the person was a relative. We established that I would call him instead, and that evening he wanted me to call him at a designated time to make sure that he would be there to answer my call. When I managed to call him, after Mother had left for her card game, he invited me to dinner the following day. I was more than happy to accept his invitation—I couldn't wait to see him again. I had enjoyed his company the day before and looked forward to hearing about his exciting life in Boston again. That evening, I had butterflies in my stomach. I fell asleep dreaming of him.

On the day of our next meeting, I called to finalize our plans. He then informed me he would be making dinner for the two of us at his cousin's home. I was flattered, nervous, and amazed that he would be cooking. I couldn't stop thinking about the evening to follow. I was so naïve then. He seemed larger than life itself and I seemed so small around him. His life was so different from mine, and much more interesting. He seemed to have traveled quite a bit and I was in awe of his grandeur. He was confident and comfortable with his surroundings, whereas I tried to crawl under a rock and hide.

When I arrived for our dinner date, he greeted me at the door with a kiss on the cheek. I felt as though I were floating on a cloud, feeling hazy as he approached so closely. I could smell his cologne, and his smile melted my heart. I was impressed that he was preparing dinner just as he had promised. He was dressed plainly, wearing blue sports shorts and a blue T-shirt. My stomach was in knots with nervous anticipation. My heart was racing, and my breathing was slightly heavy and strained. My mind raced with thoughts about how the evening was going to end. For awhile, as he stood in the kitchen cooking, I sat at the dining table and we spoke at a distance, not knowing what else to say that would be half as interesting as what he had told me previously.

We spoke about the college I was attending and my plans for the future. I told him how I wanted to be a designer, and that I wanted to move away from home some day. He wanted to know why I had chosen design as a major. I told him that because my mother wouldn't allow me to move to California to attend law school due to her fears—she thought I would get killed there, as she had seen on television. Designing was the next thing I wanted to do. He and I spoke for what seemed like forever, and we watched television while dinner cooked. I remember the table was set nicely with a bottle of wine. I also remember the look of surprise on his face when I told him I didn't drink alcoholic beverages!

The evening was going quite well, until Mother Nature intervened. I suppose all of the energy and tension between us caused my menses to erupt like a volcano. Before I realized what was happening, it was soaking through my pants. I quickly asked to use his bathroom. While in the bathroom, I agonized over telling him that I had to leave. I was hoping I wouldn't have to explain why, but when I informed him of needing to leave so suddenly, he insisted on knowing why. With complete and utter embarrassment, I told him that my cycle, my friend "Rosemary," was visiting. He insisted that I stay and offered to go to the convenience store to buy me some pads. I couldn't believe my ears! I was gasping at his offer. He was just too good to be true—too good for words. I couldn't believe his willingness to relieve me of my embarrassment without any thought of his own, to do what most husbands wouldn't do for their wives.

The attraction I felt for him had become more intense at that moment. There was no question in my mind that he was worth all the verbal lashings I would get from Mother if she ever learned of his existence. He did just as he promised and returned shortly with a box of pads. He went into a room and came out with a pair of his briefs, and asked that I change into them. He offered to wash my soiled trousers and underwear. I assumed he would put them in the washing machine located in the hall, but instead, to my surprise, he took them to the bathroom and washed them by hand. I remember feeling mortified. I couldn't believe that a person whom I had met just the day before was willing to put his hand on my soiled bloody underwear. I thought I was dreaming. I couldn't believe what I was witnessing.

That evening, we concluded our date and I went home completely blown away by his kindness. It was then, after that evening, when we secretly became—in the true sense of the words—boyfriend and girlfriend.

XXIV

REMOVING THE MASK

After months of secretly seeing each other, our relationship slowly began to change. He started to show another side of himself and I gradually adjusted my behavior and personality to suit his shifting moods. I changed in the hope of pleasing him. He told me he was the best thing that had ever happened in my life, and I believed him, especially considering all that had happened.

He said that he wanted me all to himself, so he isolated me from my family and friends, although I did see that at the time. At first, I thought he was showing me love— the kind of love I craved; the kind of love I thought was real, fueled by jealousy because that was what I was used to seeing. He had gradually asked me to stop seeing my friends. Sometimes I would give into his wishes because he wanted to be with me instead of his friends, and I thought it was only right that I did the same for him. I wanted to be with him only, as he only wanted to be with me. Other times, he would force me not to see them, but I allowed him to. Giving into his wishes was my way of reassuring him that he was the only person I wanted.

If that wasn't enough, he demanded that I not go out with my friends when they invited me. He came up with excuses why I shouldn't go. For instance, he would tell me that my friends were bad influences and would lead me astray. When I ignored his demands, he got very angry and verbally abusive. The verbal abuses were of a few choice words, but eventually led to physical abuse. Sometimes he would accuse me of being a *lesbienne* (lesbian). I would rationalized his behavior toward me and invented reasons in my mind why he acted as he did, but things never got any better. He just became more belligerent.

One day the light bulbs finally switched on. I realized what he had been doing to me had nothing to do with love at all. He had been abusive and it was really getting bad. He demanded that he pick me up from the college campus and that I had to give him my car. One day when I was waiting for him, I was talking to my classmates; he drove up in my car, but when I didn't move quickly enough to get in, he yelled out profanities at me. In a very harsh manner and in an insulting way, he asked if I was selling fish, because there were too many flies gathering around me. After I got into the car, he slapped me hard across my face as we drove away. I remember seeing stars flashing in a cloud of darkness, because he had hit me so hard.

I was embarrassed because I thought for sure that my schoolmates sitting on the benches saw him hit me. As he drove me home, he continued shouting insults at me and I had to dodge his fist many time as he aimed for my face.

That incident was the first of many others like it. All of them left me more afraid for my own safety. Gradually, our relationship was based on fear. He started making demands for me to dress in a certain way. He wanted me to wear clothes that covered my entire body except for my head. I cooperated to keep the peace between us. My body and spirit had been bruised and broken. Whatever he had minded before were now completely broken. I really wanted to believe that he loved me and that I was provoked him.

I was in a state of confusion, wondered if that was how love was supposed to be, and was supposed to feel. I wondered if that was how a man showed love. He had an extremely violent temper that he showed only to me. No one else saw that side of him. To everyone else, he was a gentleman—well-liked and well-respected, dependable and reliable. To the outside world, he appeared to be the type of young man any parents would love for their daughter—a nice, clean-cut, good looking guy from a good family.

Some of my friends thought I was lucky to have him, but they never saw the internal humiliation I felt every day, the concealed tears, or the bruises hidden under my large sweaters and long skirts. For the first time in my life, I was happy to be dark, because no one could see the marks that blended so nicely with my dark skin. If it had not been for the occasional swelling of my face, the small cuts on my lips, and red eyes from crying, no one would have believed that he had been beating me almost daily. He would always apologize afterward, kissing the hurts away, as if he could. He promised never to hit me again, but he wasn't very good at keeping his promises.

He often made threats against my brothers, and promised to hurt them if I ever thought of leaving him. He said he would take them to the pool at the local park near my Mother's home. He detailed how he would hold their heads underwater until their bodies gave way. He knew how to set me straight, though, because he knew that my brothers were my inspiration, and that they meant the world to me. I would do anything to protect them. I had seized my desire to fight for the right to own myself again, and the right to be whoever I had been before he came into my life. Though it had not been much, I needed to recognize that person again. I had become a stranger to myself and everyone else around me. Because of his threats, I was willing to face the beatings if it meant that he wouldn't harm my brothers.

Rodrigue lived in a studio apartment near the beach. One day while we were in his apartment, as he was hitting me, I fought back viciously. I had finally listened to that little voice inside my head— my mother's voice—telling me to never allow a man to hit without fighting back. I thought that was all I needed to do—to let him know that whatever he had to dish out, I would handle.

I thought about Mother's comment before. I had never had the nerve or courage to fight back and match his strength, but that day, I had prepared to fight for my life. Dead or alive, I was going to fight back with all the strength I had left in me. That day, I earned a small title in boxing. A part of me felt I was releasing all of the anger toward the men in my past. I felt I was also releasing the anger I harbored toward Mother and everyone else who had done me wrong. With my high heels in hand, I delivered the blows that my small fragile arms were too weak to do on their own. That was the first time I had worked up the courage to fi ght back, and it felt great.

To his surprise, I was as determined as he was. Each time he hit me, I laid a blow of my own with the heel of my shoe on the back of his head as he turned away from me. I went into a swinging frenzy, hitting him wherever my shoe landed. He swung back, leaving imprints of his open palm on my face. I could feel the burn on my skin and inside my cheeks. I screamed and lunged at him. I threw whatever was within my reach. When my arms were too tired and my body was no longer able to withstand his punishment, I screamed insults at him. He just laughed as if I was being silly. He knew that saying bad words embarrassed me, and he knew how to get me to stop my rage and "silly thoughts," as he called them.

I cannot recall exactly what stopped the fight that day. Perhaps it was the elderly neighbor who knocked on the door or the razor he pulled from the medicine cabinet that he promised to use on my face if I didn't stop fighting him. Maybe it was when he grabbed me by my throat and shoved me down on his bed, threatening to cut my private parts if I moved. Whatever happened that day, I felt justified about my actions, for standing up against him, even briefly.

After it was all over, I washed my face, brushed my hair, and prepared to go home. I pretended as if nothing had happened. I waited for the swelling to go down slightly and used the ice pack he had given me to cool my face and remove the redness from my eyes. During the drive home, he still felt the need to remind me that he was in control. Near my old school, just minutes from my home, Rodrigue drove my car into a light post. It was his way of showing me that he was in charge of my life.

I was scared to death as he headed toward the post. I was sure that we would both be hurt at the speed at which he was driving. He suddenly slowed down slightly near the post and jammed the right side of my car into it. After I got home, Mother asked what happened to my car and I lied. I told her I had gotten into an accident and the other person had left the scene—just as he had instructed me to say. I felt the need to protect him from Mother. If she knew what he had been doing, she would have killed him for sure with one swift move of her machete. He would be dead and my mother would be in jail, leaving my brothers alone as orphans.

I wanted to help him solve what he had told me was causing him to do those things to me. I wanted to make sure my family wouldn't attack him.

He needed me.

He told me so.

It was either life with him or the death of my brothers and me.

He told me never to leave.

He told me if I left him, I would regret it. He would kill himself, but before he killed himself, he would kill my brothers and me. I didn't want to be responsible for his hurting my brothers nor for his death. I never wanted to be the cause. I stayed with him and prayed that he would change, and that perhaps his anger toward me was only temporary. I thought that with my love, he would get better. I wanted to help him with whatever he was going through.

I protected him from Mother. Knowing how she was and knowing him as I did, I didn't want to be responsible for anything that might happen between the two. I couldn't make my brothers orphans. I wouldn't allow Mother to go to jail for his actions against me. I couldn't bear the thought of him being hurt or of him hurting Mother.

He had told me once that he was Satan's son, if not Satan himself. I believed him.

He told me he had connections that would make my family disappear.

He told me he loved me too much to let me leave him.

He told me he needed me more than my family did.

He loved me.

He told me so.

I believed him. I thought love was supposed to be possessive.

When he crashed my car into the post, I sat there; shocked that he had done it. His temper always got the best of me. Because the accident had happened a short distance from my home, I was afraid that someone who knew my mother may have witnessed the incident and would tell her exactly what had happened.

I was his punching bag.

He told me I was.

He said that I made him hit me.

He told me so.

I made him crash my car.

He enjoyed watching me cry. He enjoyed seeing the fear in my eyes. He enjoyed manipulating me into silent submission and immobility.

He had left me as he had found me before, but only more paralyzed than the walking dead in a world of motion, moving in a world that was crashing down around me, and unable to move.

I feared for myself as I feared for my brothers. They were innocent in all of my chaos. He promised if I left him, he would kill them and I would regret leaving him. They were no match for his cruelty and the brutality.

The first time I suspected that someone in my family had knowledge of how Rodrigue had been treating me was when my sisters Angeline and Ariane, my father's daughters, had stayed with Mother and me after moving from the Caribbean to attended college in Florida. It started like all the other times before—over nothing. He was scheduled to pick me up from school whenever he had my car, which was often. It was his way of keeping track of my whereabouts. On this particular day, he forgot to pick me up as agreed. After waiting several hours for him, I called home and asked Mother if one of her friends would give me a ride home. Shortly after I was picked up, he showed up, but I was gone. When he called my home, no one answered.

He drove to my house. My sisters and I were sitting at the dining room table, completing homework and studying for our exams. He walked into the room and saw me, only this time he couldn't hit me or use profanity because I had witnesses. Still, though, he expressed his irritation. I was at the head of the table with my back to the living room. Angeline was at the other end of the table and Ariane sat to her left. He walked behind my chair, mumbling under his breath about how he wanted to know how I had gotten home because he had not been the one to pick me up. When I tried explaining that one of Mother's friends had given me a ride, he was furious. I didn't want to respond to what he was saying because I didn't want my sisters to witness his temper. I didn't want them to have to listen to anymore of the insults he was mumbling under his breath.

I was very cautious in how I responded to him, how I looked at him, and how he perceived my manner to be towards him. He continued pacing alongside the table, but when he got behind Angeline's chair, he made hitting gestures with his fist and palm, demonstrating how he was going to hit me. He stopped when he suspected one of my sisters might see him. I sat in my chair wanting to urinate myself, just as I had done whenever Mother prepared to beat me. I quivered with fear and anxiety that I could no longer concentrate on studying. My hands trembled and I tried very hard to hold back my tears so that my sisters wouldn't see me cry.

He continued pacing alongside the table. At times, he stood behind my chair with his hands around my neck. He gestured for me to hurry up with my work so that I could take him home. He wanted to hurt me, but with them, there he couldn't freely do what he wanted to do. He had never hit me in Mother's home, and I was sure that he wouldn't try. When they were not looking, he squeezed my neck, and tried to block my airway. I tried to pull his hands loose with my hand, but I tried not to draw attention to what he was doing. He then stopped.

He did that several times. At one point, I heard a small crack in my neck like the sound of someone cracking a knuckle. He was applying pressure to my neck, and I grabbed his hands again, forcing him to release me. It was then that I believe my sister Angeline may have learned he was possibly hurting me. The sudden movement of my hands made her look up.

The tears were building in my eyes.

She looked at my face, and then in my eyes.

I'm not sure if she realized what he was doing, but I believed she witnessed my fear.

I was in trouble and I knew it. I thought she may have known that something was wrong just from his erratic behavior. Angeline asked me if I was okay, but I couldn't respond.

Unable to speak because of the lump in my throat, I shook my head to indicate I was fine. Deep inside, I knew that things were not okay. I wasn't fine. I thought about how I could calm him down before we headed to his home. I didn't want to leave, and I didn't know how not to. I didn't want him to bruise my body again.

When we finally left for his home, I knew that I would be his punching bag. I knew that he would hit me across my face and slap me, as he frequently did. I knew that he would hit me as soon as we turned left at the traffic light heading to his home. Just like clockwork, he never disappointed. He had his boxing gloves on. Again, I was his punching bag.

Each time, after he was done hitting me, he talked about us getting married. He told me he didn't mean to hit me and that it was my fault he got angry. All I could think of was how to get out of the hell I was in without causing anyone else to get hurt. The thought of being married to him frightened me. I visualized the beatings, his temper, and my death. We weren't married or living in the same home, yet he managed to hit me almost daily, without anyone knowing. I couldn't even imagine what life with him—alone—under the same roof would be like.

To make myself feel better about how bad things were going, I often thought about our very first date; wondering where I had gone wrong and what happened to the person who showed me so much kindness and care. What had happened to the person I loved?

I thought about the first time I had introduced Rodrigue to Mother and Stepfather. They embraced him instantly like a son. I remember the night we had invited him to dinner. He was kind, loving, and respectful. After dinner, we awkwardly sat around the table, making small talk. Time got away from us that evening. It was nearly one in the morning and Mother suggested he spend the night because she wouldn't allow me to drive him home at such a late hour.

I was astonished by Mother's kind gesture toward him so quickly. Allowing him to sleep in our home that night was totally unexpected, coming from Mother. She offered him a place to sleep with the understanding that she would also be sleeping in the same room—the living room—our designated room for the night. Mother wanted to keep an eye on both of us. She prepared a bed on the living room floor, suitable for the three of us. She spread the large comforter on the ground next to our plastic-covered sofa and layered it with additional covers and pillows. That night, in our living room, we slept with my mother between us, keeping guard.

Within six months of our relationship, many things had changed in our home. Stepfather had moved out, and Mother was under a lot of pressure to keep a roof over our heads. Rodrigue was trying to play a more dominant role. In a way, it felt as though he was trying to replace Stepfather—starting with me where Stepfather had left off with Mother. Rodrigue was no longer the happy and fun person I looked forward to seeing. His personality and his treatment of me had taken a 360-degree turn for the worse. Suddenly, I was being blamed for all that was wrong in his life.

The turn of events that followed were to everyone's dismay. In 1988, my world turned upside down, and everything crashed around me like shattered glass. I had decided that since our relationship wasn't getting any better, I wanted out for good. He had been killing me ever so slowly inside, even though I had been pretending in front of my family that things were fine between us. I decided that I was no longer going to turn the other cheek or roll over and continue to allow him slowly to kill me. I wanted to fight for what was mine—my life— although I needed to find a gentle approach so he wouldn't harm my brothers or me. For awhile, I had been mourning my impending death, wondering when would be the last time I would ever see all who were dear to me—my brothers and my family. I lived in fear wondering at what point he would finally kill me.

I thought about the things I had yet to accomplish, including my dream of being a fashion designer. I mourned it all. As long as I stayed with him, my life's outcome was very uncertain. I had lost all hope that things would ever change. I understood that by staying in this relationship, I was settling for whatever was to come. I didn't want to give in to the idea that I would probably have to spend my life—or what was left of it—with him because there was no way out. For a very long time, I suspected something was wrong with him, especially the first time he hit me. When he was with his friends, I noticed changes in his eyes, which seemed distant. He never wanted me or anyone else to question him about anything. He became angry and violent if I suggested something was wrong with him, so I stopped suggesting.

It all started making sense when Uncle Benny called a meeting with Mother and me to find out where my relationship with Rodrigue was headed. Uncle Benny informed us that he had seen Rodrigue at a place known for drug dealing. He wanted to know if I was involved in drugs or if I knew if Rodrigue had been using drugs. I was so naïve, and so oblivious to the thought of drug use. I was so naïve to the outside world; the only thing I knew of any drug was marijuana. I knew that it looked like shavings of grass. I had only seen it up close when Stepsister and her friend had tried convincing me to smoke it with them, when I had spent the night at Stepsister's house after she had gotten married (Mother had given me permission). It was while Stepsister, her friend and I were in the car on our way to pick up a food order. They attempted to get me to smoke it. When I refused, they rolled up the car windows so that I would be forced to feel the effects from the smoke. I was determined not to get involved. They called me "Miss Goody Two-shoes." My determination was so strong because I thought Stepsister was planning to get me hooked on drugs, and I wasn't going to give her that satisfaction.

Anyway, my suspicions that Rodrigue was smoking marijuana was confirmed; that a big deal and taboo in our household. I didn't understand Uncle Benny and Mother's concern, though; when they asked if I had any knowledge that Rodrigue had been smoking or using other drugs such as the "rock." I must have looked puzzled, because my uncle went on to explain that the rock was another drug, not the rocks on the ground.

Uncle Benny said he thought Rodrigue had been using "rock," based on how he had been acting in recent months. Their questioning elicited no other validation from me. I had nothing else to offer them, which would further condemn Rodrigue in their eyes. However, I did agree that he had been acting strangely.

Upon learning of the news, Mother became furious. The information Uncle Benny provided was the straw that broke her back, and the evidence she needed against Rodrigue. She had grown to dislike him for being rude to her on several occasions. She wanted me to leave him ever since he told her that I wasn't a virgin. Although, it was true, Mother did not know nor was she expecting to hear it from him in the crude way that he suggested it.

Mother found his remarks insulting and disrespectful. I couldn't tell her that what he said was true, because even at twenty-two years of age, Mother expected me to remain a virgin until I was married. She wanted me to leave him and this was her perfect reason for asking me to break up with him. I agreed with her that I needed to leave him, but I wanted to give him a chance to explain himself.

When he came to visit me that evening, I confronted him with the allegations, but he denied all of them. Mother confronted him, too, and they got into an argument. She demanded he stop driving my car if he was doing drugs on the streets that would involve me. Mother told him to stop coming around to our house and demanded that I break up with him instantly. He said something rude to her, and she put him out and told him not to return.

He became enraged that Mother wouldn't allow me to take him home. He made threats toward her and me. He came around even after she banned him from coming into our home; the two of them exchanged words again. However, this time, I was in the middle of their battle.

The next day he called without Mother's knowledge, and asked me to meet him at a local restaurant so he can clear up any misunderstanding about what Uncle may have witnessed. I agreed to meet him. Even though he was trying to control me, his own life was out of control. At the restaurant, he told me he had been having family problems—issues with his father in Haiti. I didn't believe anything he said. I sensed there was more than he was telling me.

He wanted me to feel sorry for him, and I did. He also told me that he wanted me to run away with him because he thought that my family—meaning Mother—was influencing me to leave him. He said he had been planning to move to Texas and he wouldn't leave without me—not without a fight.

I loved him and I wanted to help him and not abandon him, but that wasn't going to happen in Texas. Not with me, alone with him. If anything was going to work out between us, it would have to be in Florida.

Several days later, he showed up in front of our home again. He waited for Mother to leave so that he would see me and convince me to run away with him to Texas. When I refused him again, he shoved me. Unfortunately, when Mother returned home later that evening, our neighbors reported what they had witnessed between us. That was the first time anyone had seen him put his hands on me. They told Mother and she told Uncle Benny. Both were now on alert, waiting for him to come back; Mother waited with her bat. He learned that everyone was on the lookout for him, so he stayed away for a short while and kept a low profile.

I saw him only sporadically, I wanted to let things cool off before I broke up with him. He was unstable and I knew his state of mind, therefore, I didn't want to trigger any unwanted reactions. Mother continued to demand that I stop seeing him. If I didn't, she threatened that she would rather send me back to Haiti than to allow me to bring shame to her door. Then she was insistent on knowing if I was pregnant with his child.

I refused to give in to Mother's demands. I was twenty-two years old and I wanted to make my own decisions. I couldn't tell her that he had threatened the boys and that I was planning on leaving him. I told Mother the decision would be on my terms, when I was ready. This was my third brave attempt to stand up to Mother, and she didn't like that at all. In a way that only Mother could pull off, she decided to teach me a lesson about disobeying her once again.

The next thing I remember was that she was lashing out at me, then she headed toward the hall closet to retrieve the piece of wood she was saving for anyone who got in her way. Unfortunately, that day, that person in her way happened to be me.

That night, Mother gave me the beating of my life. Worse than when she had beaten me with the umbrella; Mother grabbed that piece of wood and laid it into me. We were tussling while I was trying to get the wood away from her, she grabbed me by the hair and pulled chunks of my hair out as she attempted to pull me across the floor. As with previous beatings, I knelt in a fetal position to shield my face from the wood in her other hand.

Each time I forced myself down on the floor, Mother tried to pull me up by my hair. I tried sandwiching myself between her and the floor. I remained on my knees, praying, pleading with her to stop as she pummeled me with all of her strength. I screamed in pain and agony, there I was at twenty-two years of age; being badly beaten for disobeying my mother's wishes.

During the beating, my sisters Angeline and Ariane attempted to make Mother stop. To protect me, they jumped between us to help shield me from the blows that were coming my way. Mother shoved them out of the way. They pleaded for her to stop beating me before she killed me. I heard the fear in their voices. They were afraid for me. The beating was so severe on that horrendous day that I felt the warmth of urine trickling down my legs again just like before. After Mother was done, all I could do was crawl into my bed to ease my aches and pains.

My decision that night to stand up for myself, wasn't about Rodrigue. Instead, it was very much about my attempt to break free from Mother's control. I refused to leave him based on her selfish demands. I refused to make her issues with him my issues, because I didn't see the two as being the same. Therefore, I gladly accepted my beating and felt free from both of them.

Mother, as usual, ordered me to take a cold shower to ease the swelling. My sisters helped nurse my aching body. For days afterward,

I was unable to walk properly. My body was stiff from the trauma. I was engaging in an internal war with myself and with everyone around me. The entire ordeal had been too much for me to handle alone, but I wasn't about to give up. I didn't want Mother to think she had won, because she hadn't. I remained firm about my decision for wanting to leave him on my terms.

In my heart, the relationship was already over. I had made up my mind. I had a chance to salvage my dignity and pride, and nothing either of them could have done to me then would change my decision either way.

He had done it all.

Mother had done it all.

The situation was still very delicate and I had to handle it with care, because I knew what he was capable of doing. He was unstable and I was concerned for my brothers' safety.

He still called periodically, hoping I would change my mind and run away with him. I usually tried to change the topic. One day, though, I couldn't ignore him because he was insulting me every chance he got. I finally told him that it was over between us and he shouldn't call anymore. I told him we needed to be apart to give us a chance to clear our minds because so much had gone wrong between us. I said my good-byes.

He wouldn't take "no" for an answer. Later, he arrived, driving my car, which he parked in front of my family's house. He wanted to talk. Just as I had done in the past, I listened, feeling sorry for him because he was alone. I had made a mistake in judgment by allowing him to use my car. This time, though, was supposed to be the last. He said he would return it before I left for school the next morning. I let him take the car home, because I didn't want to leave with him, and I was afraid that I might not return.

The next morning, he didn't show up. I wanted to give him another chance, but he didn't want one for himself. I managed to get a hold of him by telephone. He nonchalantly said that he was keeping my car for ransom in the hope that I would change my mind about leaving for Texas with him. He added that if I wanted my car back, Mother had better pay him for it.

Mother called Uncle Benny, our family enforcer and told him what had transpired and that Rodrigue accused Mother of owing him money. I told Uncle that he wouldn't return my car until Mother paid him. Uncle Benny was upset that he had to spend his time looking for Rodrigue. However, he knew exactly where to look.

Within hours, Rodrigue was driving my car home, with Uncle Benny following behind in his own car. After Rodrigue had returned my car, he requested that I take him home. Uncle refused and told him to leave.

Rodrigue refused to leave until I had told him to his face that it was over. So in front of the small crowd of people who had gathered around, he asked if I wanted our relationship to be over. I told him that I did. He was visibly upset and embarrassed that I had broken up with him. He asked me to open the trunk of my car so that he would get something out. There, in my trunk, were all of his clothes, and all of his belongings. I supposed it was embarrassing for him to remove his unpacked clothes from the trunk, while everyone watched on. Uncle Benny then liberated me from Rodrigue's control by handing him $400.00 and arranged a ride for him to his destination, but not before he promised that he would return, because until *he* said it was over, it wasn't over.

XXV

KIDNAPPED

The breakup wasn't as amicable as I thought it would be, but I felt lucky to have Uncle Benny to help shoulder my burdens. It was great feeling comfortable with myself again. In the days that followed, Rodrigue called nonstop, making demands and threats. For days, I wasn't able to go to school or work out of fear that he might be waiting for me along my route. When he called, he'd tell me he was on his way to get me. The neighbors had warned Mother that they had seen him wandering about our home, watching it. I knew he had been upset but thought he would get over it soon.

He kept his promise, though, and tried to control me even after the breakup. One Thursday evening as my sisters and I sat in our room, he tried entering our window. We could hear the window crack as he forced it open and tried to push through the screen. My sisters and I screamed until Mother came running into the room. When he saw Mother, he ran. She took off after him with her machete, with neighbors joining her in the chase.

Afterward, I sat there shaking, on the edge of my bed. I couldn't believe that he had possessed such nerve to try to force me to leave with him. Not much later, Mother and nearly half of the neighborhood returned from the chase. Some stood in front of our house. Mother said she was disappointed he had gotten away. We called the police and reported the incident. An officer arrived to take our report and advised me to keep a low profile because no one knew the state of his mind. The officer also suggested that I file a restraining order against him. He explained to me what that was and why I might need one. I contemplated whether I needed to file the report, but decided against it. I didn't want him to get into more trouble. I thought calling the police would be enough to keep him away from me,

During that entire weekend, I was a prisoner in my own home. I avoided any activities outside because I was afraid he might turn up. I wanted everything to go back to normal. By Monday, I decided to return to school with renewed confidence that it was all finally over. I thought for sure he wouldn't come back again, because everyone was on the lookout for him. I decided not to hide anymore. I wanted to feel free and alive again. I didn't want to dwell on all the times he had beaten me. I didn't want to linger in thought about where he might be or what he might be doing. I didn't care where he was. I just wanted to go back to school. I remained cautious nonetheless.

Monday afternoon, after one of my college classes was over, I headed straight home, wary of all the cars around me. I looked over my shoulder to make sure he wasn't lurking about. Luckily, I made it home safely. By then, I was overly confident that he wouldn't return. Shortly after arriving home, Mother asked me to go to the local supermarket for her. I was more than happy to take the ten-minute drive from our home, and brought along my eighteen-month-old niece. On the way, I took a slight detour into the parking lot of a pharmacy. Just after I had pulled in and was turning to open the car door, there he was, standing on my side of the car. He was pointing a gun at my head. On the other side, another man stood next to the passenger door.

Rodrigue demanded that I unlock the doors and get into the back seat. After he and the man entered the car and realized that my niece was there also, the two agreed to drop my niece home, because they didn't want to go to jail for kidnapping a baby. When I heard their plan, I quietly placed my small change purse, with my driver's license, in her jacket pocket. I held her tightly as they drove back to Mother's home. When they got there, Rodrigue asked some kids who were playing outside to take her to my Mother. He then drove away.

The entire incident was surreal. They told me to lie on the backseat so that I wouldn't see where they were going. They didn't want anyone to see me, and they didn't want me to signal anyone. I had no idea where they were taking me. They made several stops at various telephone booths. They instructed me to call Mother and tell her I had been kidnapped and was being held for ransom. He told me to tell Mother to call my Uncle Benny and ask him to put up the money for my release.

When they finally allowed me to call Mother, her suspicions were confirmed. She had known something was wrong when the neighborhood children had handed her my niece. I told Mother the words, just as they had instructed me, and I told her that she didn't have a lot of time. Rodrigue and the man hurried me to the telephone because they didn't want the call traced by the police. When I called Mother again, I learned that detectives were at our home. They got on the phone and I told them that the two men who had me wanted money from Uncle Benny. The detectives asked me other questions that, for my own safety, I couldn't answer. After that call, the two men ordered me to put my head down on the backseat and to keep my eyes covered. They permitted me to look up only when they stopped so that I could make a call. The locations were unfamiliar. I didn't recognize any of the landmarks.

Each time I called, the detectives wanted to know where I thought I might be. I didn't know. They asked that I remain calm and told me not to worry. I was frightened because Rodrigue held the gun to my side during those calls, so no one would see the gun as he walked close to me towards the phone booths. As I spoke to the detectives, I could hear Rodrigue talking in the background about how he was going to make my uncle and Mother pay for breaking us up. The tears welled up in my eyes, but I couldn't cry, and I tried my best to suppress them.

I was then driven somewhere else where the two picked up a third man. That man climbed into the backseat with me. They handed him the gun, which he held to my head. As we drove, all of us heard the sound of a helicopter, which we presumed was trying to track us down. They stopped again so I could make another call to Mother.

I thought I was having a nightmare. I didn't want to believe the latest turn of events. During one of the calls, the detectives negotiated an arrangement whereby one of the two other men would pick up the ransom money. I relayed those instructions to the three men. The plan was that the third man Rodrigue had picked up would leave to get the money. After he had returned, they would set me free. One detective cautioned me to listen carefully to his instructions. He told me what would happen after the man had returned and said I wasn't to repeat his instructions if I wanted to return home.

Back in the car, Rodrigue asked me what the detectives had said. I told him that the money was ready. Within twenty to thirty minutes after the third man left, Rodrigue and the other man made me call Mother to see if the third man had picked up the money. Just as the detective had instructed, I told them that the money had not been picked up because the third man had never showed up. They cursed angrily, speculating that the third man had chickened out at the last minute and gone home.

At that point, after going over their plans again about how they would share the ransom money, they decided that, of the two of them, the second man would finish what the third man hadn't. I prayed that they wouldn't change their minds about who would stay behind with me. I prayed I wouldn't be left alone with the second man. He seemed to be the most committed to killing me if things didn't go as planned. If I were left with him, I was sure no one would ever find my body.

Before the second man left to get the money, the two of them spoke about what would happen if they were caught. If the authorities threatened to arrest them, would they go down fighting with their boots on, like cowboys? Again, they discussed shooting me and dumping my body somewhere in the water with alligators, perhaps in the Everglades. Each time I heard them mention killing me, I wanted to take off running, but I had nowhere to go.

They drove to another location so the second man could take a taxi to Mother's home to retrieve the ransom money. They thought that if they had me call from one location and then they drove to another where the man would be picked up by the taxi—thus mixing up the locations—the police wouldn't be able to trace the calls or link the second man to the kidnapping.

Again, when I made another call to check on the second man's arrival, the detective—just as before—assured me that no one had arrived to claim the money. Throughout the ordeal, I had been the translator for my own kidnapping—the voice between Rodrigue and the detectives. Rodrigue thought as long as the police couldn't identify his voice, they couldn't pin the kidnapping on him (or so he believed).

On the final call to Mother to check again if the second man had arrived, the detective again informed me that he had not picked up the money. Rodrigue became suspicious that this was all a setup and someone was making a fool out of him. I was at an advantage because I knew the police had arrested the other men. Now, I just needed to figure out how to get Rodrigue to let me go. I was grateful that Rodrigue was the one left behind with me, although I was aware that my ordeal wasn't over. He still had a gun and threatened to use it on both of us.

He drove in a big loop from one end of town to the other. I thought that my life would be ending when he drove into an open field, turned off the engine, and sat in the dark, thinking about what he would do next. In my mind, I began to plan how I would manage to fight my way out, and I became even more afraid. The awkward silence between us was broken when he turned on the interior light and removed some of the bullets from his gun. He then held the gun to my head and told me that he had two bullets left—one for me and one for him—and that if he couldn't have me, no one else would.

My brain immediately went on autopilot as I tried to figure out how to calm him and keep him from shooting me. I instantly catered to his feelings of wanting us to be together. I told him I would do as he wanted and I'd go wherever he wanted. He asked why I had abandoned him when he needed me. He wanted to know why I had embarrassed him and humiliated him in front of my family. I said that I had no choice because Mother had beaten me. I hoped he would understand and not shoot me. I pleaded with him not to shoot. I told him that he didn't really want to go to jail.

I begged him not to shoot either of us, because I knew that he would then have to shoot me first. I told him that I would run away with him if he would put the gun down. I kept him talking about his plans for us. The more we talked, the calmer he appeared. He eventually laid the gun on the floor next to his feet and drove out of the field. He had changed his mind about killing me, but he was angry and drove at mad speeds. He drove so fast, I thought he would crash the car. He zigzagged down the roadway, and sped into an area with large homes and very few cars along the road. He drove so fast that he hit a curve he hadn't seen, and the car became airborne. It landed in the middle of the street, and crushed the gearbox.

He was unable to get the car started again. After pondering the situation, he decided that we had to get the car off the road, so we pushed it into a parking lot next to what I thought was a gas station. We got back into the car and sat while he contemplated his next move. He said he was sure the police would stop to check on the broken-down car. In case they did question us, he instructed me to tell them that we had both been kidnapped by two men who had fled after crashing the car.

I wanted him to trust me again. I agreed to tell the police exactly what he wanted. His next move was to remove any trace of his involvement with my kidnapping, including the gun. We walked down a sidewalk, not far from the car, and he threw the gun over a wooden fence into someone's backyard. We returned to the car as if nothing had happened and sat inside in full view of other passing cars. He had me rehearse what he wanted me to say when the police arrived. He wanted them to believe that we both had been kidnapped.

Many hours seemed to pass before a police car drove up and flashed a light into the car. The officer who approached us was a female, and for whatever reason, I was afraid for her and me because I didn't know what Rodrigue would do. I was afraid he would try to grab her weapon. She approached slowly and asked for our identification. I told her that I didn't have any, and Rodrigue appeared very nervous. The officer wanted to know how the car had ended up with all of its tires blown. She asked us to get out of the car. I began to cry and hoped that she would be able to handle his temper. I hoped he wouldn't try to take her gun, especially because earlier, he and one of the men had talked about going down fighting like a cowboy.

His arrogance got the best of him. He told the officer the rehearsed kidnapping story and about how the car had ended up where it was. Because I was wiping away my tears, though, the officer wanted to know if we had been fighting. I was unable to speak. I wanted to answer but the words wouldn't escape my lips. I couldn't bring myself to tell the officer all that Rodrigue had instructed me to say. I didn't want to lie to a police officer.

Finally, all I was able to say was, "Call my mother. She'll explain everything."

With a puzzled look on her face, she finally realized that perhaps I was frightened of him and was afraid to speak. I continued to ask her to please call my mother so she could explain.

The officer returned to her car apparently to check by radio if my car had been reported stolen. My thoughts were so hazy that I hadn't even thought of telling her that the car belonged to me. She returned with her gun drawn and ordered Rodrigue to lie face down on the ground. Another police vehicle arrived to assist. As she questioned me, a male officer came over. She told him that Rodrigue and two other men had kidnapped me and that police had already arrested the other two men. The female officer was furious, perhaps because Rodrigue had lied to her. She cuffed him and placed him in the back of the other officer's car.

I was relieved that I didn't have to lie to either officer. I was relieved that they knew exactly what Rodrigue and his friends had done. I was happy that I was still alive. As the officer placed Rodrigue into the backseat of the police car, he shouted that he was sorry for not shooting me when he had the chance. He said that he promised he would get me for not speaking on his behalf and not telling the officers what he had instructed me to say.

I rode in a separate police car to police headquarters, where I would need to identify the other two men involved in my kidnapping. My mother and friends met me at the police station. I was grateful to the officers and my family for all they had done to get me back unharmed. I was so happy I had not been harmed. Even though I had already felt free of Rodrigue before my kidnapping, my freedom was now confirmed because he was going to jail.

The kidnapping had put a strain on my relationship with Uncle Benny, and things after that were never the same. He told me he was glad I had made it home safely, but other than that, he didn't speak to me about the incident again. He became more distant and less visible in my life. I wished I could have done something to eliminate that distance between us. Uncle Benny stopped coming over to our home as much. Even when I called him, he was slow to respond. I understood that the kidnapping had changed everyone and he needed to process the incident in his own way. Uncle Benny clearly had become angry with me, and understandably, so I thought. I was disappointed in myself for disappointing him and for shaming Mother. Although everyone had been very nice after the incident and treated me like a broken doll, I hated feeling vulnerable again. I hated seeing the pity on their faces and hearing it in their voices. I hated feeling pity for myself. I wanted to feel strong and I wanted to know that my life would forever be different.

My thoughts about my life suffocated me. I felt as if it had been unstable, and I wasn't quite sure where I was headed. At twenty-four years old, I had lived a life full of disappointment. I wanted a chance to do it all over again—to live with laughter in my heart—but as long as I remained in Florida, my happy dreams would remain tarnished.

Mother had been having her own issues at home and my heart was breaking for her and my brothers. The pressure on me to help support them was overwhelming. It was difficult being their caretaker for so long, and although I still loved Mother despite our differences, I couldn't continue to live under her control. Since the kidnapping, Mother was more protective than before, demanding more of my time, and required feelings from me that I couldn't provide. Stepsister had her own family and since Stepfather had moved out earlier, Mother was left with all of the responsibilities, most of which had become my own. For years, I had filled in as a mother to my brothers, and with Stepfather gone, I helped Mother financially by working a part-time job while attending college full time. I was drained of energy. My life seemed burdensome, and I was on the verge of a nervous breakdown.

I decided that to save what was left of me, I had to leave home. The following year—after completing my two-year college degree—I planned to go somewhere safe, anywhere but Florida. Although I didn't want to break my promise—to protect and take care of my brothers— it would be detrimental to them and to me if I stayed only for that reason. I wouldn't be able to help them or myself. I realized that I needed to be in a neutral and healthy environment. Living under my mother's roof and control wasn't conducive to healing. I also needed a place to hide. I feared that Rodrigue would have someone else finish what he had started. I constantly looked over my shoulders. My trust in people had been shattered and I was in desperate need of an overhaul. My friends tried to help me regain some of what had been lost, but my life had been too severely fractured, and my energy was seeping out. I couldn't see past the trauma I had experienced. I was trying to keep a positive outlook on life but it was difficult, especially when everything around me seemed depressing and disparaging.

I determined that my refuge would be Alaska. I knew that Mother would never visit there because of the weather conditions, and even if she did, the visits would be short and infrequent at best. I wanted to get as far away from everyone as I possibly could. After the incident, our relationship had improved somewhat, but it was still strained in many ways.

The year I graduated, I decided that instead of moving to Alaska, I would move to New York. I had made my decision after Mother had visited New York. After her return, I swore that every cold she had thereafter had been the result of the snow flurries falling on her head in New York. She swore that she wouldn't visit there again. My plans were sealed. I would move to New York. I reassured myself that I wouldn't see much of anyone from my life in Florida.

When I told Mother of my decision to move to New York, she was in denial that I would ever have the courage to live without her. She thought I was so dependent on her that she didn't believe I would leave or be able to make it on my own. Even after I purchased my airline ticket and packed my bags, Mother was certain that I would change my mind. I knew that I couldn't continue to live in Florida with all that had happened. I couldn't allow Mother to discourage me. The week leading to my departure, Mother was dismayed. The family and our neighbors were trying to guilt me into staying.

They asked what Mother would do without me; how she would survive if I wasn't around to help her with the household responsibilities; and how my brothers would get on at home and in school without my guidance. I spent a lot of time contemplating my decision to leave. I had thought about the outcome beforehand, but I couldn't afford to lose this fight. It was something I had to do for my sanity.

I fought for everyone else for so many years, and just this time I needed to fight for me. In June 1989, I moved to New York with only $500.00 to my name, hoping never to look back. My cousins and auntie there helped me by allowing me to live with them in their studio apartment. Life in New York came with hope and possibilities. I got a job as a bank teller and made only about $17,000 a year. I called and told Mother. She thought I was making a lot of money, as did I at the time. I didn't care about the money, though. I was on top of the world because I no longer had to look over my shoulder. I was happy working, making my own way, and living with family.

The bank offered many exciting experiences I had never had. I was exposed to people I had only seen in magazines and television. Although I felt small compared to them, my eyes were being opened to new possibilities. I loved dressing up and going to work rather than standing on a street corner selling my body or having multiple children from various fathers, as Stepfather had once predicted. I took advantage of everything offered. That August, I enrolled in a business college to pursue a new degree in business. I was no longer interested in fashion and was unwilling to do the groveling to get ahead in that industry.

In many ways, school had been my one refuge from my world and my past. I enjoyed interacting with the other students and I enjoyed the challenges, even though I struggled to keep up. I had been on a quest to prove to everyone that I was intelligent and capable. I wanted to prove to everyone that I wouldn't be running back to Florida should things become difficult. Going back to Florida wasn't an option for me. My heart wasn't there and everything I knew about it had become strangely unfamiliar.

New York provided me with a sense of freedom I had not felt in a long time, and my life was good even though I was living in poverty. Looking back, if anyone had told me I was poor at the time, I would have argued with him or her. I never felt impoverished. The thought of being unfortunately poor wasn't part of my vocabulary. I understood that if I worked very hard things would eventually get better. I never allowed myself to feel self-pity because I didn't have something. I knew if I worked hard enough, I could attain what I wanted. If there was one thing I learned from my mother, it was that she was very resourceful. I shared my mother's resourcefulness. I knew how to hold my head high, no matter what the circumstances. With that in mind, I had the time of my life just being silent and at peace with my thoughts. I felt I had been given another chance to enjoy life and another chance to get it right. Nothing else would get in the way of that.

XXVI

EVOLUTION

I had fallen in love once again. It had been nearly three years since my tumultuous breakup, and I was now living in my own apartment, and I wanted to give love another try. I felt ready to trust again. For the first time in my life, I dated other people without thinking that the date was an invitation for marriage. I became comfortable with the idea of not having to marry the first person who showed an interest in me or was kind to me, as I had been taught while growing up.

At first glance, he wasn't the type of man who would pique my interest if I spotted him in a crowd. However, as the saying goes, never judge a book by its cover. I felt blessed and lucky that I had taken the time to read the pages a little while longer.

He and I met, strangely enough, through a mutual friend—a classmate who had promised to set me up on dates with his football friends. Jack frequently told me that he had found me the perfect man, but that perfect man never materialized. This time, though, Jack was on target. He introduced me to the love of my life. After our writing presentation class period had ended, Jack approached me and promised that *this time* he really had found the perfect man for me. As before, I indulged his enthusiasm, mostly because I enjoyed listening to him speak. I never really gave much thought to his suggestions. Deep inside, I was afraid of the unknown, and of not having control over the type of person he might see fit for me. I didn't like the idea of being set up with someone I had not met myself beforehand.

Jack was so excited about me meeting his friend that the more he talked, the more interested I became. He said he would meet with this friend the next day and he asked if he could give him my telephone number. I agreed. The following day—a Wednesday, if I recall correctly—after I had returned home from school, I found a message from Jack's friend on my answering machine. His accent sounded strange. I couldn't place it. It was nothing I had ever heard before, yet his voice was appealing. The message was that he had called at our mutual friend's suggestion. He asked that I call him back when I returned home that evening. I was excited, captivated, and mesmerized by his voice. I couldn't wait to speak to this stranger.

When I called him back the following day, I left a message. It wasn't long before he returned my call. I was impressed by that. We spoke for hours. He had a calmness about him that transcended the telephone—so much so that I had forgotten I was at work. I couldn't believe we had spoken for so long on my employer's time. Later that evening, we talked by phone again, and he invited me out on a date. I accepted his invitation to go on my first blind date with my new European friend.

On Saturday, he arrived at my apartment to pick me up for our date to see a movie in Manhattan. Earlier, I had called my cousins and told them about my upcoming blind date. I gave them his information in case I didn't return by the time I told them I would be home. I didn't want to be too careless. Although he sounded pleasant over the phone, I couldn't trust that he wouldn't hurt me. My experiences had taught me plenty about people and how not all experiences turned out pleasant.

The buzzer to my apartment rang. With great anticipation, I walked down the hall to the front door of the building and let him in. He entered and followed me to my apartment so I could retrieve my purse. He complimented me on the size of my home and how tidy it was. As he led the way to his car, I remember checking him out from behind. The view was very pleasing! I liked the way he walked. He seemed like a manly man—well-packaged in all the right places. At the very least, I would feel safe and protected in the streets of New York City with this man.

To this day, I can still remember the scent of his cologne, what we both wore, and more profoundly, how we got terribly lost trying to get out of Queens and into Manhattan. While he tried to find his way through the maze called Queens, we talked about everything, yet nothing. It didn't matter that we were lost for what seemed like hours. Just listening to him speak was enough to make me forget that. His voice was soothing and time just seemed to drift away.

He finally managed to get us to Manhattan, and we headed straight to the movie theater. He held my hand as we crossed the street—not too tight and not too loose. The firmness of his hand gripping mine comforted my soul. I remember the day precisely, because it was the release of *Sister Act*. Inside the theater, he held my hand throughout the movie. I felt warm inside, as if we had met before this day and he was a long lost friend from the distant past.

After the movie, we headed to a nearby bar for a drink. It was exciting going into a bar. I had been to clubs, but never a bar. Since

I didn't drink anything other than ginger ale, I settled for that and enjoyed our conversation. We discussed just about everything under the sun, from my school, to my job at the bank, to my part-time job at one of New York's elite department stores. After our date, he drove me to my apartment, where I thanked him for a great evening.

The following week, he invited me out on another date, a new adventure—a day trip to visit upstate New York's Bear Mountain. Although I didn't particularly like spending time in the great outdoors, I was happy to experience hiking for the first time. During the entire drive there, all I thought about was snakes and bugs. I tried to be very brave in front of him.

At that moment, I felt life couldn't get any better. That Friday morning, we were out exploring nature, and, unbeknownst to him, he was helping me face some of my fears of the outdoors. I especially remember our walk up the trail toward the top of the mountain. It was the perfect setting—the calmness of the trees, the perfect shades of green, and the various colors of the leaves. I experienced a feeling of peace and oneness with nature that I had never had before. As we slowly walked up the trail overlooking the trees, we threw small rocks to see which of us could throw the farthest.

The view was picturesque and serene. It was there, on top of Bear Mountain, that I heard the whisper—the sound of a soothing voice telling me that he would be my husband. I heard it, but I wasn't sure if I had heard what I thought I had heard. Then there it was again! I felt strangely uncomfortable thinking that here I had just met this man and now I was hearing a voice whispering that he was going to be my husband! I wondered if I was losing my mind, yet a feeling of complete peace washed over me. I never knew or realized such peace existed. My mind felt clear, and my heart lighter. I didn't share this news with my new friend, because for one, I didn't want him to think I was losing my mind, and secondly, I didn't want to scare him away after only our second date. I trusted in the whisper and decided to be completely myself—no eagerness to impress, no need to be accepted by him, no need to be possessed by him or for me to possess him. I felt extremely happy and joyous. My heart was smiling.

It had been nearly two months since we had met, and I was forging ahead with my decision to move out of New York—a decision I had made before we met. I was still on a quest to find the quietness my soul had been seeking. In August 1992, I packed my bags and moved. With his encouragement and with uncertainty of our future together, I left New York without any regrets. That was the first time in my adult life when I had felt confident and certain with the course of events in my life. I wasn't concerned that he wouldn't be around. I believed in my heart that the voice I had heard on the top of the mountain would guide me. I believed he was the one for me. I believed that whatever the universe had set forth would be.

In just a little over a year, we were married in a small, private ceremony with friends and family. Fourteen years of marriage and two children later, he is still the love of my life, my best friend, and my soul mate—chosen just for me.

For a long time, I accepted that we were meant to be together. Our relationship was peaceful, but something inside me wanted to jeopardize all of it. I felt undeserving of someone like him, and although we had been married for nearly ten years with few marital incidents, I began doubting the love I had for him and the love we had for each other. I looked for ways to shake the calmness of the ground beneath our feet, but he never wavered. His love and commitment to me and our family remained strong, even though my own commitment felt questionable. He did whatever it took to assure me that he wasn't going anywhere. Nevertheless, I couldn't help but fight against it. I wanted all that he represented to be false. I craved the chaos that I had been accustomed to most of my life.

Over time, the dark shadows crept in again. It wasn't enough that he loved me if I didn't love myself. I couldn't see and appreciate him for the person he was until I learned to appreciate myself. His patience and love brought me back to the place where my heart longed to be—to a quietness and peacefulness, that was my own. I knew I couldn't have picked a better man on my own. The universe had intervened and selected him for me. Despite my demons, he loved me unconditionally—with all of my flaws and imperfections.

For years, I tried hiding from my reality, not wanting to admit how my past pains and suffering had affected me. My denial was insurmountable. I thought that once I had married and given birth to my own children, all the hurt would vanish. The erosion of my emotional stability became very apparent after the birth of my first child. I felt selfish for bringing a baby into my world and thinking that a child would be the answer to my unhappiness. That was so far from the truth. The hurt had never left. Instead, it had lain dormant and restless. Not until my daughter got older did I understand how deeply I had been wounded, because that wound manifested in my daughter. As my little girl grew, it seemed that just the sound of her voice would trigger my mood swings, along with so much anger; anger that I never thought I had in me. I had violent thoughts about both of us. I thought about not wanting her to go through the pain I had gone through. I wanted to protect her from the world I had experienced, and the world that had destroyed my trust in people; the world I felt I wasn't part of, and the world that was still very frightening to me.

I have never felt as unstable as I did on that one particular day. I learned I was expecting and was so excited. I spent nine months of motherly bliss preparing for the day of her arrival. However, because my baby was overdue, the doctor would have to induce labor a week early, so Mother arrived early that week. She wanted to make sure I received proper care after arriving home with the baby, as it was customary for a mother who had just given birth to receive a proper bush bath to help with the healing process.

Everything was going according to plan. The day of my scheduled induction of labor had gone smoothly. After my baby was delivered, my world turned upside down.

It all happened so fast. I remember holding my new baby and looking at her beautiful face. Her eyes were closed and swollen, but she was an absolute angel. Just as we were getting acquainted with one another and I was looking forward to spending my life being the best mother I could be, the fight for my life began. The details are still vivid in my memory—the mood of the delivery room and the look on everyone's face when the gushing sound erupted; the splashing of blood on the floor like a scene from a horror movie, as if someone had committed a horrible, bloody crime; and the stunned look on my husband's face. The nurse took my baby away and I blacked out. I went in and out of consciousness and felt completely numb. I heard my doctor tell my husband with great urgency that I needed a blood transfusion, and that I might have to have my uterus removed. So much happened within that short time.

Even in my critical state, I mustered up whatever strength I had left to fight against receiving a blood transfusion. I mumbled to my husband and the doctor that I didn't want a blood transfusion, because I was afraid of contracting AIDS. I was afraid of dying. I asked the doctor to test my husband or someone in my family as a viable match for my blood type.

Lying there on the hospital bed feeling helpless, I worried what would happen to my baby if I weren't around to take care of her. Throughout the mayhem, I felt as though I were subconsciously praying, asking God to give me another chance to hold my baby, to guide the doctor to make the right decision, and to help me get through this tough and uncertain time. I prayed that God wouldn't make my daughter an orphan and my husband a widower. In a profound moment I'll never forget, I saw a white, glowing light surround someone who was floating over me and looking down on me. The image was as an angel in a bright light who was making sure I knew everything would be fine. Later on when I regained consciousness, the delivery doctor said he couldn't understand what had gone wrong. I had arrived at the hospital healthy and then, suddenly, death was looming in my corner. I had suffered heart failure and water had filled my lungs.

I was so sad when my daughter went home without me because I had to remain in the intensive care unit. Mother, my husband, and my best friend, Solange, cared for my baby until I came home. Mother stayed longer than planned, but shortly after my release from the hospital, she left. I cried, wanting her to stay longer, feeling for the fi rst time that I really needed her. I had not felt that way about Mother's presence for a long time. I felt vulnerable, and unprepared to care for my new baby on my own.

All went on with their routines as I slowly spiraled downward. I can never replace the support of my dear friends who helped me overcome some of my demons. I'm forever grateful to Solange for being there with me in my time of need. She took over and helped me. She was also there for me when my husband was at work. Solange became my life force. She gave me moments of reprieve and an escape from my darkness.

The nightmares I was having were slowly killing me. I couldn't do enough to rid myself of those thoughts and feelings. I became more obsessed with washing and bathing to rid myself of the memories. My desire to feel clean at all times had never changed. I thought that, somehow, I could wash the thoughts away. Behind the shower curtain, I felt safe. I could wash away my tears without anyone wanting to know or asking why I had been crying. I wanted to wash away the dirt, the filth *they* had left behind, and the remnants that were forever crawling on me. But the images never left my mind. For years, they raped and molested me. They violated me without regard for my feelings, and without regard for my age. I was only a child.

Now, with my own daughter, my rage burned brightly. I was unable to deal with that burning rage that had flared up inside me as I tried to cope with my anger and shame. I rationalized why *they* had done what they did to me. I justified in my mind that their crimes happened so long ago, that it was time for me to get over the feelings and memories. Inside, I was slowly dying, and slowly decaying in self-destructive thoughts. *They* had claimed my innocence, but I was unwilling any longer to allow them to rape and claim my soul, my heart, or my mind.

For many years, I mourned an internal death—the death of my inner child. I wasn't able to speak of the death, nor could I reach out to anyone who may have been able to help me cope with my loss. I never thought it was something that would require that I get professional help to deal with what had happened. Alone, I mourned the loss of an innocent child who had fallen victim to *their* violence. Every day, the tears rolled down my dark face. I have cried rivers.

The tears didn't stop rolling down my dark face.

There were invisible ones and quiet ones, like the quiet whisper of a mild wind.

The tears never stopped.

I cried every day of my life, and even when my face was visibly dry, my heart wept. The nightmares haunted my soul and the tears became my companions and provided me solace. The sorrow and heartbreak I experienced were unbearable. I could rarely remember being able to function without the fears or without the tears. I felt incomplete. They had become my safe haven, and allowed me peace and solitude of mind in a world of chaos and confusion.

The tears had cleansed my shameful soul, cleared a path through the darkness, and purified and washed away my doubts when my purpose for being on this earth seemed unclear.

The tears had always flowed as a river down my face, and it was time I allowed the sun to dry them. It was time for us to part.

XXVII

SECRETS REVEALED

I will never forget the day when I became free of my burdens, and the day my load became lighter. Over the years, I had rehearsed in my mind how I would tell Mother about all of the terrible deeds our so-called family and friends had done to me in her absence. No amount of preparation could have fully readied me for that day. With all my careful planning, none could have predicted the outcome. In an instant, it had all changed.

The confession to Mother happened so quickly and strangely. It wasn't at all how I had envisioned it—never over the telephone— and her response wasn't as I had imagined. The hurt and suffering I had endured had new meaning for me. I wasn't sure how I could have expected Mother—in one conversation—to alleviate a lifetime of pain. I had held on to my images of this conversation for so long, and suddenly, I had no time to prepare my lines. I had no time to rehearse the delicate manner in which I would speak to Mother. I wanted to make sure I didn't come across as accusing or blaming Mother for my problems, and for not protecting me when I needed her most. I had imagined the perfect scenario of how I would begin the conversation, what I would say, and how it would end.

For more than thirty years, I had waited for this opportunity, and it had arrived this very day in 2005—the day after Thanksgiving. My telephone rang; it was Mother, calling to wish me a belated Thanksgiving. I was happy to hear her voice, and although our conversations were usually very short—two- or three-second routine calls at most—she generally managed to leave me laughing about something or another. Today, Mother and I were both very happy and felt good because of the holiday. Today, Mother was bubbly and in very good humor.

She asked about the kids and my husband, as she normally did during our calls. I hadn't expected that we would talk for as long as we did—about nothing as usual, making small talk about the nieces and nephews in Florida to fill the void between us. Then, suddenly, Mother described the problems she had been having with her blood pressure. She joked that her doctor had suggested a cure for her high blood pressure. She needed to find a boyfriend. I knew she was kidding, but a part of her sounded serious. I could tell by her tone that she had been contemplating her options. We both laughed and joked about the doctor's recommendation that Mother engage in sexual pleasures to release her pressure! In fact, I laughed so hard that my stomach hurt.

I was still laughing as Mother continued telling story after story. At one point during our conversation, Mother talked about my brothers' strong opposition to her having a male companion. She mentioned that they had been giving her a hard time about a previous relationship and wouldn't consider any suitable male companions from within her circle of friends. One of her reasons for calling was to inform me that she wanted my approval if she ended up finding a suitable partner.

I was flattered that she was seeking my approval, but I told her the decision was hers, not mine or anyone else's, to make. We discussed Mother's resistance to bringing anyone my brothers might object to into her life or her home at her age. I was certainly entertained by her story. Mother went on to say she would consider only two men in her circle of friends as companions, and she made justifications as to why she wouldn't want a partner at this point in her life.

By then, she had piqued my curiosity. I wanted to know who those prospects might be, although I had already guessed one of them. Mother told me the name of one of them. I wasn't surprised, although I briefly felt ill prepared for that news. I was taken aback, hearing his name mentioned again after so many years. It was as if an electrical bolt had surged through my body. I knew Mother had no knowledge of her friend's crime against me, but I couldn't help feeling betrayed, wondering why she would still consider him a suitable companion. When she blurted out his name, I felt as if my heart had stopped beating. All the joy I had been feeling on that holiday dissipated and turned into fear and horror. My body was paralyzed.

I felt nauseated and nervous at the same time. My knees buckled, but I held firm, leaning against my kitchen stove, and using the countertop to brace myself. I wanted to scream, but the sound wouldn't escape my lips. My chest tightened. I was suffocating. I took small, slow, shallow breaths to calm myself down. At that very moment, I wanted Mother and the world to know that he, her potential companion, was a child molester, and a rapist. I wanted to scream, "HE'S A RAPIST!" but the words wouldn't come out.

I felt betrayed by Mother and by myself for not having the courage to speak out. I listened intently—but said nothing—as Mother continued talking about him. From that point on, the conversation felt labored. All I could think about was that I had to tell Mother the truth, but I couldn't find the courage. The mention of his name, and the thought of my long ordeals with him, sent cold chills up my spine. My fear and disgust made my hair stand on end.

I attempted to change the subject and asked Mother who the other suitable companion was. I had hoped to move on from my frozen state. As Mother continued talking, my thoughts again drifted to him—Uncle Gabriel. The memories came rushing back. Nearly three years earlier, he had attended Uncle Benny's funeral, and I had unknowingly been standing across from him in line to enter the church. His gaze pierced through me like a hot-iron rod. At first, I didn't recognize him—the blackness of his hair against his weathered and aged pale skin threw me off guard.

Mother had always spoken so highly of him, and now I stood to discredit the one person she had idolized for so many years. I wondered how I could tell her that the man whom she idolized had molested and raped me while she had entrusted our care to him.

I needed to know his whereabouts. Fearing him had drained me, and even though I knew he would no longer be able to cause me physical harm, I wanted to know what had become of him since our paths had last crossed at my uncles funeral. I asked Mother. She explained that he had recently died in a jail, for assaulting his son, but she didn't know much else. Although, I did not expect that news! I was surprised to learn of his unfortunate demise. I felt relieved.

I had been afraid of him ever since the raped me in the Caribbean, and even though I had seen him many times thereafter in Florida, the time that chocked me the most was again, when I saw him standing next to me on the day of Uncle Benny's funeral. After seeing him, I felt a cold chill run across my body because of the way he was looking at me. Tilting his head; as if wondering if his eyes had betrayed him. Our eyes met, and I quickly looked away from him. I couldn't stand being next to him, but I couldn't leave either. With his gaze, he was violating me all over again. I was quite distraught that he was at my uncle's funeral. After the service was over, I left quickly and called my husband to tell him about my encounter with one of the men who had raped me. My husband was one of two people with whom I had shared details of my past.

After hearing from Mother about his death, I celebrated it in my mind, because I now knew he could never hurt me again. I felt guilty for wishing death on another person, guilty for wanting him dead, and guilty that his death was necessary to free me from some of my shame. Perhaps his death was my cowardly way of dealing with my pain. Perhaps it was my inability to confront him in person for devastating me and destroying my life. Perhaps the news of his death and the circumstances surrounding it were more than I thought he had deserved. Nonetheless, I knew I would never have an opportunity to confront him in person. More importantly, I was no longer his prisoner.

That evening, when Mother and I said our good-byes on the phone, I still had not revealed my secret. I wanted to tell her about the suffering he and a few of her friends had inflicted on me over the years. Yet, I realized that even after all of these years, as an adult in my own right, I was still afraid that Mother would blame me for what they had done. I didn't want to face Mother's disappointment or feel the shame of it, and I didn't want to relive the pain with her.

After placing the receiver down, I felt the urge to call her back to tell her. I wanted to clear the air between us. I needed to get the monkey from my back. I needed to tell Mother all about the dirty, filthy secrets they had forced on me. I wanted her to experience every detail of the pain I had gone through. I wanted to break free from the guilt I had carried since I was ten years old. I wanted to tell someone about the strange conversation I had with Mother. I wanted to tell them how I felt somewhat unburdened for the first time since learning of Gabriel's death. I wanted to tell them how the layers of my troubles were slowly peeling away.

I ran to the basement, where my husband had been working, and related the details of my conversation with Mother. He encouraged me to call Mother back to tell her about the rapes and the molestation. Nevertheless, as I had often done in the past, I resisted and recited many reasons why I couldn't tell her about my painful memories; why I needed to protect her feelings; and why I must spare her from having a possible heart attack because I didn't know if her heart was strong enough to withstand the load of my past. I told him I didn't want Mother to become ill or suffer a heart attack on my account. She was better off not knowing.

The truth of the matter was that I couldn't stand her *not* knowing. Throughout the years, I thought about what it would do to her if I told her. I thought it would destroy her, and I thought that she wouldn't be strong enough to handle news of such magnitude, to handle the guilt and shame as I had. I still wanted to protect my own feelings from Mother's reaction, too. I still needed to come to terms with issues I had not yet resolved. I convinced myself I would destroy her with my confession. I needed to find the perfect time to tell her, when we were together, face to face.

I told my husband that relating my story to Mother over the telephone wasn't part of my plan. I told him that I couldn't tell her until the following summer, when I would visit her. I wanted the time and place to be right and perfect for both of us. I wanted to prepare myself.

I was afraid, because the only other person other than my husband I had shared my horrific truths with was my Auntie Angel, the mother of one of the men who had molested me, and she ended up dead from a broken heart. I blamed myself for Auntie Angel's death. I felt responsible for not keeping quiet. Perhaps she might not have died of sadness and a broken heart if I had not revealed that someone dear to her had been doing unspeakable acts against me.

As I said those words aloud to my husband, my thoughts were screaming, "Tell Mother! Tell her! Tell her! For the sake of your children, tell her!" Suddenly, I felt a greater urge, and a greater need to confess. I felt that if I waited any longer, I would miss another opportunity to confront my past.

On that day after Thanksgiving—the evening of November 26, 2005—I went into my home office and confronted my fears for the first time since many years ago. I lifted the handset from the receiver, dialed Mother's number, and made the dreaded phone call. Mother answered. She sounded surprised to hear from me again so soon. She asked if everything was okay.

With my heart pounding and racing, I told her that everything wasn't okay.

It all happened so fast. I told Mother I was calling back because I had something that I needed to tell her. She hesitated, and waited. She asked what it was. My voice trembled with fear, but I continued.

I said, "When we spoke earlier, you mentioned Gabriel's name."

"Who?"

"Gabriel."

"Yes."

"Well, hearing his name brought back a lot of bad and awful memories."

"Bad memories?" she asked in surprise.

"Yes. Bad memories," I responded.

"Why bad memories?" Mother asked.

"They're bad because of the things he did to me when we lived in the Caribbean—the way he often touched me, and the awful things he did to me."

"He touched you?" she asked, bewildered.

"Yes," I responded. "Yes. He did bad things to me many times."

Mother echoed, "Many times?"

I proceeded to explain in minor detail, asking questions to help her recollect events of years past.

"Do you remember when you asked him to look after us sometimes when you were out playing cards with your friends?"

"Yes," Mother responded.

"Remember when I had just come from Haiti?"

"Yes," she said again.

"When you were out playing cards sometimes…"

Mother then cut me off from my "French Inquisition" and said, "Yeah, yeah, when you came from Haiti."

"Yeah, that's when he began doing those things to me."

"What did he do?" she asked.

"He touched me and did lots of things to me."

"How did he touch you?"

I tried to find the words to describe what he had done. I tried explaining in our native Creole, but, although I switched between English and Creole, I couldn't find the words. I felt that Mother wasn't getting what I was trying to explain to her. I didn't have the vocabulary, though, to explain in Creole. Even with our communication barrier, I was determined to get this over with once and for all.

Then Mother asked, "Did he try…?"

"He touched me. He did things to me, and he forced himself on me several times."

Again, she asked, "Did he try…?"

"Yes, he did. He touched me many times."

I still didn't have the heart to tell Mother directly that he had raped me. I couldn't utter those words.

The tears began to build and then slowly streamed down my face. I tried to maintain my composure. I felt the shame all over again. The memories and the scars were all too real to deny.

Mother sensed my tears, and she spoke in a soft tone, almost whispering, as if the wind had been knocked out of her, "Why you crying for?" she asked, in her broken English. "Stop crying and get yourself together. Stop the crying!" she demanded, as if ordering a child.

Suddenly, I felt as if I were a child again being scolded in public for doing something wrong. I was afraid to speak and stand up to

Mother. I was still trying to find the right words to say to avoid getting a verbal lashing, and to keep from hurting her feelings.

"How come you never told me?" Mother asked.

I was unable to compose myself enough to reply, so she continued. "I would make sure the mother f----er never did it again!"

I finally replied, "I never told you because I was very afraid of you. You made me afraid to tell you anything. I was afraid to speak."

Then Mother said, "You tell me too late. It's a good thing the mother f---er is dead. That is why I get my machete; I bought a machete when I married your Stepfather, to protect myself. You should tell me then."

"Mom," I said, "my stepfather never touched me or did anything like that to me."

"I know," she replied. "He would be dead. I would cut his head with my machete if he did that. If you tell me when the mother f---er is living, I make him pay with him life."

"He's a mother f---er to do that to me," I said. "I trusted him and he betrayed me and my confidence."

Mother asked again, "How come you never tell me that?"

Again, I replied, "Mom, I didn't tell you because I was afraid. He told me he would hurt me if I said anything about it to anyone. I was scared."

I added, "You made me afraid of you. I could never talk to you about anything. I was afraid to tell you because when you and your friends spoke of things like this happening to girls, you always talked about what you would do to me if I shamed or disappointed you. I felt ashamed, and your friends would say it was the girl's fault if something like that happened. I always thought it was my fault. That is why I never told you."

In Mother's own silent rage and torment she said, "Okay, okay! Don't cry. Don't think about it. Don't talk about it anymore. Don't talk about it to anyone. It happened long ago. It's in the past now. You don't need to think about it no more. Don't talk about it. Keep it secret. No one needs to know. You keep your secret, I keep your secret, and we don't talk about it. Don't tell anyone."

I remember saying, "Mom, that's not all of it. There's more."

"More what?" she asked, in a tone of anger mixed with surprise.

"There's more I need to tell you."

"More?"

"Yes."

"More."

"I still have more to say. He wasn't the only one. It happened many, many times."

"Many times?"

"Do you know why I never wanted you to give Cousin Thomas my telephone number after I moved away when he asked you for it and about me? Well, that's the reason I never wanted to talk to him."

"You mean him, too?"

"Yes, Mom, him as well. Do you remember when you would go out and give him the keys to our apartment to check on us at night? That's when he did it."

"What he do?" she asked again in her broken English. "He touched you, too?" she asked in disbelief.

I said, "Yes, he touched me and did other things."

Then she asked, "How he touched you?"

I began to explain, and again my eyes filled with tears.

I could hear the change in Mother's breathing on the other end of the receiver. I could feel her torment. I sensed her motherly tears, but once again, I felt I needed to protect her from the pain—protect her from the gory details of so many years ago.

Slowly and cautiously, I said, "He did similar things to me as Gabriel."

I didn't go into the details of what Gabriel had done all those years. Neither of us was ready to handle the full details of those horrors, so I continued.

"Thomas touched me and he did…"

She interrupted, "When he do them?" as if to question my recollection of events that played out in *my* life.

I said, "He did it when you left him in the apartment to watch us, and when you gave him the keys to the apartment."

I continued to answer Mother's ongoing questions.

"Sometimes after he was in the apartment watching television, when it was time for me and the boys to go to bed, I would ask him to leave. I locked all the doors behind him, but somehow he got back into the apartment. Several times, I caught him. I asked him to leave and put him out again. I locked the doors and checked the windows, but he always managed to get back in.

"He came back while the boys and I slept. In the middle of the night when he knew you or Stepfather had not returned home, he came into our room and touched me as I slept. The first time it happened, I awoke and he apologized and then left. As time went on, he did it again and again. I don't know how he was getting back into the apartment. I couldn't figure out if he had a spare key. Even when I took back his key, he found a way in.

"One night, I remember waking feeling strange, as if someone were watching me. I quickly jumped out of bed because I felt someone touching me. He was standing over me. Most of the time, I thought I was having a bad dream, but it was him. Another night, I woke up feeling a sticky wet mess on my nightgown. There he was again, standing over me with his penis in his hand. I was afraid of what he had done to me while I was sleeping."

"Who was in the room with you?" Mother asked. "Was anyone else in the room with you?"

"Yes," I said. "It all happened during the time the boys and I shared a room. They were sleeping in the big bed and I slept on the small bed next to the window."

"Did the boys see anything?" Mother asked.

"Mom," I said, "I don't know if and what the boys saw. They never talked about it with me. It was dark, late, and I can't tell you what they saw, but I don't think they saw anything—they were asleep."

The French Inquisition continued.

I said to Mother, "I would ask him to leave but he would come back."

Her angry compassion rang loud, "Why you don't tell me this? Why you don't tell me so I take care of the son of ma beech? You should say something. I kill him. He be dead now. Chop the mother f---er head and go to jail. Go to prison for life for killing a mother f---er."

"Mom," I said, "that's why I couldn't tell you. I was afraid you would beat me and kill them. I was thinking about the boys. I knew you would want to do that. I didn't want you to go to jail because of me."

I continued to justify why I had not told her.

"The two of you were friends. I didn't want to cause any trouble between you and him."

Frustrated and diligently restraining her tears, Mother responded, "That no friend, no friend like that. You trust mother f---er and mother f---er betray you. No friend, that no friend."

"Mom, that's why I asked you never to give Thomas my telephone number, I thought I could deal with the situation on my own. After moving away, I felt safe. I didn't want to speak with him ever again. I wanted to forget about everything. That's why I was upset and surprised when he called me that Sunday night."

She continued with her silent anger, "The mother f---er always ask me for your number when he call. All the time, she said, I make excuses, telling him I can't find my telephone book; tell him only one person has the number. I tell him when I need to talk to you, I ask the person call for me. The mother f---er always asking me for your number. What he think, the mother f---er?"

"Well, Mom," I said, "he called me that Sunday out of the blue while Sylvester, the kids, and I were having dinner. The telephone rang, and when I realized it was him on the other end, I was angry. I thought you gave him my telephone number. I couldn't speak to him at that moment. I told him I would call him back. Even though I didn't stay on the phone for long, the kids knew something was very wrong. They asked me if everything was okay."

"Sylvester asked me who was on the phone," I continued, "and I told him. I couldn't eat anymore after that. He had ruined my Sunday dinner with my family. Hearing the sound of his voice after so many years had made me furious.

"When I decided to call him back that evening, I felt angry and confrontational. I wanted to confront him for the first and last time. I wanted to confront all of them. I wanted him to know that I knew now what he had done to me back then. I resented the fact that he thought I would be happy to hear from him. I hated the way he sounded happy at my expense on the other end of the phone when I picked it up, as though he were my friend, when I had lived in fear of this moment, and in fear of him.

"As I redialed his number, my hands were trembling, and my heart raced in a panic. I felt both nauseated and anxious because of what I was about to do. The telephone rang and he picked up.

"'Hello?' the voice on the other end said. It was him."

"With a stern, nonchalant voice, I asked, 'May I speak with Thomas?'"

"'This is Thomas,' he said."

I responded by saying my name.

"While gasping for air, I quickly said, 'I'm calling you back for two reasons. The first one is to ask how you got my telephone number, and secondly, to ask you never to call my home again.'"

He sounded surprised by my request and abruptness. He told me that he had gotten the number from one of my family members. Then he asked why he couldn't call me anymore.

"I was furious that he would question my reasons for not wanting him to contact me. Angry at his question, I reminded him not to call my house because I never wanted to speak to him.

"In a stunned and stuttering voice, he asked, 'Really? Why?'

"I said, 'Yes, really! I don't want you calling me. I don't have anything to say to you.'"

"He continued to ask why."

"Again, I said, 'Because of what you did to me when we lived in Florida. Because of all the bad things you've done--as if he needed reminding."

"Reliving the ordeal, I felt it was my responsibility to clarify things for him, as if he had forgotten it all.

"I was enraged that he pretended not to remember what it was like when he molested me. I had not forgotten. In fact, I had lived with every detail of those many nights for a long time, and I'm still living with them. He had no right to forget how he had ruined my very existence.

"Angrily, I said to him, 'You molested me. Don't you remember? Do you not remember all the nights when Mom trusted you and asked you to keep an eye on us? Do you not remember that I would put you out of the apartment and you would come back in afterward to touch me while I was sleeping? What about all those nights I woke up to find you watching me, standing over my bed with your penis in your hand? Do you not remember any of it? I don't care if you don't remember. I do. That is why I don't want you calling my house. I trusted you and you broke that trust. You were like an older brother to me. But you betrayed me, my mother who trusted you, and our family. I was fifteen and you took advantage of all of us.'

Stuttering, he said, "'I know what you're saying, mama, but, but…'"

"I blurted out, 'But, but, nothing! I know you remember what you did, because I do.' I abruptly placed the handset on the receiver, hoping never to hear from him again."

As I replayed for Mother the conversation between Thomas and me, her response was simply, "Good! I'm glad you told him. That is why he was punished. That is why he had a stroke and now he is a cripple. The people you trust are the ones who betray you."

Then I said to her, "There's more."

"Still more?" she asked.

"Yes, mom. There's lots more, so much more. Do you remember when your friends came to our apartment and I never wanted to be around them? Do you remember that?"

"Yeah," she responded.

Then her words hit me like a brick.

Mother said, "It's history. Forget it. Don't worry about it now. Don't feel sad or sorry for yourself. Nobody needs to know this."

I sat in my office with my mouth ajar, trying to come to terms with what Mother had just said, but I couldn't wrap my mind around it. I couldn't believe what she was telling me. I couldn't believe that, now, when I was truly ready to speak of their crimes, she was trying to silence my voice again. I couldn't believe that after all the years of waiting for the perfect time and thinking that she would understand my pain, it had all come down to this.

Mother said, "You married now. You have a nice husband and two girls. What happened is in the past now."

Mother's words cut through me like a sharp knife. My body froze, and once again, I felt betrayed that Mother would ask me not to speak of their crimes.

"Mom," I said, "I have been living and thinking about their crimes for a long time. I can't just stop thinking about it now."

"Well, you better try," she said, as if it were an order—an "or else."

"Don't tell anybody," she said. "It's our secret, and no one needs to know."

Like the frightened child I had been at age ten, I agreed. I agreed not to speak of their crimes anymore—at least not with Mother.

It was tragic that after all of those years, Mother couldn't understand or feel my pain. Perhaps her own shame had caused her to want to hide. She couldn't understand my heart, and I realized that it wasn't my job to make her understand the trauma I had endured over the years. The secret was out, and one thing was certain—I would be silent no more.

XXVIII

A LETTER TO MOTHER

I have stood in your shadows for hoping to be noticed, recognized, and loved. I have stood in your shadow not for the things that have gone well in my life—my family, children; but for the shame I have labored to keep hidden all those years out of fear that the little inkling of love you may have had for me would not disappear if you learned what those men had done to me.

However, as I became older, I saw in you a mystery that couldn't be solved; a woman I had not understood and when I became a mother in my own right, I still hid in your shadows, frightened, struggling not to be as you were with me. What I realized over the years, though, is that if I take away the few minor inconveniences and the difficult challenges of your life that you were trying to control, when I take away the horrible times, I realize that I am very much like you in so many ways, even I can't deny. The differences between us are the paths you laid out for me, which were not part of your own experience. Your generous and your giving, caring heart for your fellow man and woman and helping other children in need have always fascinated me. What I remember most about you was witnessing how you would share your last grain of rice with a perfect stranger, how you would provide shelter to some of the neighborhood children in need, even though our space seemed overcrowded still astounds me.

Looking at myself in the mirror, I see you looking at me and me looking at you. Although my fears of never wanting to be like you was not unusual in my mind—and though that would be the fear of most daughters—I have spent nearly three decade trying to avoid what was inevitable. Over the years, I have come to accept that it was impossible to chase away the history, the qualities we shared so deeply; and impossible for anyone to spend as much time with another person and not emulate them in some way or another.

What I have also learned was that I didn't get to where I am today without your struggles and your sacrifices, however unfair I may have thought them to be at the time. Today, I share and display some of your greatest attributes and cultivated qualities that I have admired most and discarded the less desirable ones. I found that when I put the pieces together—as painful as some of the experiences were growing up—when I really allowed myself to see your true beauty, your struggles and truest intentions, your truest heart, you were a mighty force.

I have come to terms with the notion that there isn't any one perfect human being on this earth. The truth is that we all have imperfections, though most of us like to think otherwise. My fears of you were more of fears of the unknown—I never felt as if I really knew you until I allowed myself to discover you; knowing your own past and our circumstances.

In my heart of hearts, I know now you were trying your best to survive in a place where your life and well-being meant nothing to anyone else, except to those who loved you. I understand that as strangers and foreigners in an unknown country, you wanted so much for us to seize the opportunities that were in front of us, to be able to accomplish what wasn't within your own grasp.

I couldn't see past that present moment, when all you were attempting to do was navigate our future with what you had to work with. At the time, I didn't understand your convictions and fierce determination to provide and survive. Your relentless push for us to succeed was daunting, and the result of your own ill education.

You never showed fear or weakness in your quests. Your determinations to get us over the imposed hurdles were, at times, overwhelming, your fierce words and that no-nonsense, in-your-face approach of raising us sent chills down our spines, but you were on a mission.

So often, I was caught up in my world and experiences that I never really saw your struggles to give us everything that you had to give. I didn't allow myself to see the great qualities you possessed, the richness you have passed on—not monetary wealth, but richness and an abundance of qualities and love for others. My fears of not wanting to be like you were overshadowed by my thoughts of the crimes that were done to me, that I felt you should have protected me against. I have released my fears of you because those thoughts no longer hold true. They no longer hold me prisoner, keeping me from enjoying what life has set before me.

Today, I understand your history a little more than before, the history of the many great women like you on whose shoulders I now stand. I stand in the realm of forgiveness—of you and of myself. I welcome the stream of forgiveness to wash over both of us like clear rain on a bright, sunny day.

Such forgiveness is not as much about the past as it is about our future—yours, my own and my daughters. My heart and soul hungers for it; through the years, I have harbored so little forgiveness and ill thoughts of you because of the things that had happened in my life that I felt you were responsible for. Now, I want to rid myself of the hurt, self-loathing, self-pity, pain, and hatred toward others. I know that I must seek forgiveness in my heart for those people who have harmed me so deeply, in order to see the beauty in you and around me. In my quest for the truth in my life, I have also realized that my purpose on this earth is not to harbor hatred of the past, but rather to find meaning in all the experiences that were sent in my direction.

I know that God didn't make any mistakes when he set out my path, because I know that he wouldn't put me on a path without a plan. The lessons were much too great, not to be grateful for them, no matter how awful and cruel some of them seemed. Those experiences have helped to instill strength and determination in me and a desire to do right.

As I search for truth, peace and love in my life and for my own children, I know that the search must start within me. I must forgive others for their shortcomings, so that I may be at peace within myself and accept my own shortcomings. I have considered how much you accomplished on so little, all the efforts you put forth to give us all that you had to give—and all that you are still giving, providing the best way you knew how. My thoughts of you have evolved over the years and I can only dare to walk a mile in your shoes. I can only dare to be the wonder that you are—to possess your wonderful qualities that I hold dear; qualities that have shaped my life.

Despite your own obstacles, you still stood victorious, giving of yourself freely to anyone in need. Your wisdom continues to grow and given a different time and place, a different set of circumstances, you would have moved mountains; which in my mind you have.

I have admired your kind and gentle nature when the storms in your heart were not brewing. I have admired your generosity for taking in and feeding those less fortunate than you, always offering them a place to rest and a warm plate of food to feed their souls; and always sharing even if it meant you had to do without.

I have loved you like no other. You are a survivor, smart and resourceful, and even though your intelligence didn't come from a textbook, the lessons you taught me came from your own experiences and wisdom. I have learned about your inner beauty and your strength and I wanted to let you know that my admiration of you hasn't gone astray. My admiration of you, once a secret in my heart, has made its way to the surface so that it is readily available whenever I fall short of my own aspirations.

I no longer blame you for the things that had threatened to destroy me. No longer will I blame you for the things that have gone wrong in my life, because to continue to blame you would be the denials of the underlying gifts you have bestowed on me. I elevate you, because without your push, direction, and sacrifice, I wouldn't know my own strength. Today, I understand that given your own circumstances, you couldn't always be there to protect us, to protect me. I understand that your desire to put food on our table and keep shelter above our heads was much greater than your pride.

Today, I stand with the understanding that a mother will walk to the ends of the earth when her family's wellbeing is threatened or jeopardized, as ours had been growing up. Something that has always amazed me was that you were able to send five children to Catholic school on a four-dollar-an-hour salary, while managing to keep a roof over our heads.

Your resourcefulness continues to baffle me, but then again, knowing you as I do today; you would not have expected anything less from yourself. I never heard you complain that it wasn't enough. You accepted your limitations and made do with whatever you had. You managed to turn four dollars into twenty-four or more just for a chance that you might give us a better life. I'm grateful that you saw a way out for us through education, and staked your life on it. I now understand your vision—that as a foreigner in a country that discredited you and expected you to fail because of your nationality, which you used to fuel your fire.

Even when the situation seemed dismal and grave, you wouldn't welfare to be your temporary solution because you were afraid of the impact on our future. You taught us to stand on our own merits and to earn our way. When we had no food on the table and no lights to shine our way, and when you weren't sure sometimes where our next meal would come from, you never relinquished hope and determination.

I have forgiven you for being gone those many nights and days, not knowing when you would come back home. I now understand the risks of facing the unknown, holding out a bit longer hoping you would hit the jackpot and be able to feed us for another day, or have just enough for the next school tuition. I have forgiven that we didn't understand each other, for being so full of dislike for the essence that was you, and for our inability to communicate as most mothers and daughters communicate. I have forgiven you for never telling me how much you loved me until it was almost time for me to leave your nest. Perhaps I would have looked at life differently, and perhaps things between us would have been different. However, I never doubted your love, even when your actions stated otherwise.

As I stand here today, a mother, I now understand your fears and for making sure you provided for your children the best way you could. I admire your determination to want everything to be right for us. You wouldn't let anything stand in your way of accomplishing your wish for us, even though another approach may have presented a different result. I understand that your lessons for us stemmed from your own experiences. Growing up, I loved and loathed you, because that was all I could do.

Today, I choose to love you instead. Much of my energy has been wasted in blaming and hating; those wasted energies have become overwhelming and exhausting. I love you because you are the better part of me, strong and kind, even though some of the qualities you displayed were less desirable and their impact on me nearly detrimental. I will forever keep your truest heart to share with my children and grandchildren hopefully to come.

I appreciate your wisdom and resourcefulness that have guided my life, because you never saw yourself as others saw you—a poor, ill-educated Haitian woman. You never saw yourself as poor even with your limitations. Thus, I never saw myself as poor or allowed myself to think poorly of my dreams or aspirations. You have given me the greatest wealth of all, the kind not signified of money and that no amount of money can ever replace.

Although, you may not possess heirlooms to pass down to me, or my children; to give my them some idea of their lineage, and even though you do not possess monetary wealth to provide as inheritance, what you have passed on to my daughters and me is so much more—what you've passed on are your strong Haitian values, a women who will not settle for anything nor allow anything to keep you from seeking opportunities for a way out.

The greatest lesson, the greatest wealth that you have passed on to my daughters is that they are strong and must use that strength to rise above any unfortunate circumstances whenever their lives seem to spiral out of control. They will come to find strength and courage in your journey and in mine

I have learned that to forgive someone, is not to forget the past; but to find peace in the world. I have learned from you that everyone deserves a chance; I am open to giving both us permission to take that second chance.

I love you still and always!

Think!

Think carefully.
Think hard.
Think forward.
Choose your path wisely.
Choose the path within you.
Choose to make your own experiences.
Learn from your journeys.
Choose the latter and ride the waves to a better destiny!
Calm the storms inside and the motion of the waves will be more enjoyable!
Let your inner compass shape and dictate where you land. Do not go gently into the past because everyone deserves a second chance.
Think!

Adera

EPILOGUE

Today, my mother and I share a mutually respectable and loving relationship. Since leaving home, she has never attempted to tell me how to live my life or how to raise my children. She has been nothing but loving, supportive and always happy about my accomplishments.

My mother still lives in Florida and is the proud grandmother of nine grandchildren ranging between the ages of twenty-one to six months old. She continues to be a pillar of hope, strength and sacrifice for many of our family members and friends in need; and since having grandchildren, she has transformed into a different person all together. Her views on child rearing have changed from the hay days of when my brothers and I were growing up.

In her role as grandmother, she has become a gentler force, contradicting the past. Sometimes, thinking about the person she is today and the person she used to be makes me laugh. Remembering how she raised us with an iron fist, it was hard to understand the one time I called her for some motherly advice about my oldest daughter, how she was totally against spanking her. Hearing her on the receiver telling me that I needed to be patient; I remember holding the telephone away from my ear, wondering if I was speaking to the same person who used to kick my tail.

Before moving away, Mother and Stepfather were separated, but have been now for nearly twenty years, although they have not legally divorced. He still lives in Florida and has been living with the same girlfriend since leaving us. Currently, Mother have been supporting three of my stepsisters' four children for the past seventeen years, with no financial support of any kind from her; their biological fathers or grandfather. She has managed to care for her grandchildren, while working seasonal part-time employment; and the occasional assistance from my brothers and me. Mother still believes that her luck will change one day at playing bingo and cards in hopes of hitting it big.

My stepsister still resides in Florida, our relationship is nonexistent and her whereabouts are unknown. My brothers are adults and two of which have children of their own, all three of them are still trying to survive in a community that continues to oppress them.

As for my abusers, the men who drastically and forever changed the course of my life. Well, two of them there whereabouts are unknown and assumed dead, and the other currently lives in New York. He has attempted on several occasions to make contact, but his last attempt was in 2005.

I am grateful and happy for my family and truly blessed to be with the man I am with today, my husband! From the moment he learned of my journey, his feelings for me have never wavered, he continues to love and support me every day. He has supported me in writing this book; supported me in coming to terms with my truths, and has been my biggest cheerleader.

My daughters are wonderful young human beings, looking at the world with new lenses, but the lessons I learn from them daily, never seizes to amaze me. I have learned so much from them, admiring their strength and determination to see good in everyone through forgiveness and in working together.

About the Author

Adera Gordon currently lives in Maryland and shares a home with her husband and two wonderful daughters.